THE TROUBLE WITH KIM

On Transcending Despair and Approaching Joy

Seth David Branitz

Inter*Section* Press

An imprint of Ridgeline Creative Services

https://www.ridgelinecreativeservices.com

The Trouble with Kim: On Transcending Despair and Approaching Joy

© 2020 by Seth David Branitz

ISBN: 978-0-578-80713-3

Library of Congress Cataloging-in-Publication Data

InterSection Press is an imprint of Ridgeline Creative Services, 174 Huguenot Street, New Paltz, NY 12561

The Trouble
With Kim

This book is dedicated to Martha Morenstein
who once called me a writer.

Thank you Liam McAllister for taking an interest in this
project and for outwitting my complacent tendencies in
order to drag this book to completion.

To the wonderful writers in my life and
the many brave storytellers at The Moth, TMI Project,
Woodstock StorySlam and beyond, who show me
how its done.

To Eve, Henry & Kim Branitz for giving me life, loving me
a lot, and for making me laugh now and then. It's always
a treat when we meet in my dreams.

Thank you, Jenn for your love and for the room to do
my work, and to our sons, Jules & Harper who adore
and uplift me, even when I'm gone.

And to you. May you know how vital your story is.

TABLE OF CONTENTS

INTRODUCTION

I have a friend who calls herself a happy carrot. She says that some people are just naturally content, that the lens through which they see the world brims with goodness, and that it doesn't take much for them to feel secure. They consider their problems, deal with them, and get back to the pleasant business of being alive.

I know a few who are beneficiaries of such a blessing. They adapt easily and make the best of the very same world that brings others to their knees. They believe that things happen for a reason. They're bright and lovable and their performance reminds the rest of us that there's a chance.

Happy carrots, my friend says, have a good sense of humor and are fun to be around. They think about good things that have happened, and are excited about better things to come. They live more easily in the moment, and aren't at the mercy of time constraints, always rushing off to get somewhere. Happy carrots are already there.

I am not a happy carrot.

The messages from my upbringing included equal parts, "There's something very wrong" and "Don't tell anyone." This left me few options.

Seth Branitz

I was poor, hypersensitive, sickly, and in close quarters with my small family, chock full of dead dreams, mental illness, and cockroaches.

I was also white in America, richer than some, able bodied, intelligent and had access to medicine, school, art supplies, and a guitar. I lived with both of my parents, and had locks on the front door. I know that many others don't have these advantages. I don't pretend that my struggles were more severe than others', or that having passed those particular obstacles wouldn't have been made harder if I were—for example—black.

But I think we all have stories that are worth telling. For my part, I think that the bulk of my experience would be wasted if I hadn't decided to revisit it and brush it off for the page.

When I began the process of collecting mental snapshots of my past to write about, the memories manifested like fireworks. I started to tell them at live readings and story slams, and posted a few on social media. I added a story or two between songs at gigs. The feedback—the relating—was clear enough to make me write more.

The time I spent in my stories with family and friends who've since died felt precious. These had become ghosts, but now I got to be back in relationship with them, if only for seventeen hundred words at a time.

The stories in this book revisit the very helplessness that dominated the early part of my life. I wanted to explore my memories of a life that I'd thought had been haunted with bad luck—and wasted on poor choices—with an open mind. I wanted to make it better for my younger self, and assure him that it wasn't all his fault, that even when it was, he was still worthy of love, and that life is good.

What I found, however was that whereas these events had come and gone, for the most part I'd moved on to the next pressing matter without allowing the effects to sink in, I was now reliving each scenario—in slow motion and with critical attention. In some cases, I believe that I felt the old experiences for the first time. I dug them up, aired them out, and saw them for what they were. If I'd known then that this exercise would sting and depress me to the degree that it has, I would have stopped before I began. I ventured into a distant but familiar hell where I have no power to affect change or redirect fate. It's done, but I dove deeper, and while I found the players in my immediate family more reprehensible than I'd previously reckoned (myself included), I now see something I had no idea would manifest; forgiveness. I'd carried around a universe of resentment and blame. I hated anyone associated with my failures and misdeeds, whether via blame or envy. But digging in and then stepping back has afforded me the chance to see that they—we—are all hurt, lonesome and remorseful.

I see how different I am from them, and how similar. I'm no happy carrot, but have a growing affinity for joy. I'm exhausted from carrying the soggy and tearful weight of the world. I'm ready to share the load.

By way of a trigger warning I'll just say that the essays include a few frank descriptions of sex, suicidal ideation,

Seth Branitz

suicide, moral and mental illness, death, and sexual violence. I thought about creating a key with coded markers for the pieces that include each of these so that you can navigate the collection from the comfort of your personal boundaries.

I haven't gotten to it.

— *Seth*

FAR ROCKAWAY, 1968 - AGE THREE

THE WORLD WAS soft when I was three.

My dad, Henry, adored me, but he didn't let me color on the walls. I still did it as often as I could, knowing that it upset him and Mom. I couldn't resist the specific delight of a drawing there as opposed to on designated surfaces.

My mother, Eve, had always lived in or at the edge of poverty and I think that's part of why she took such pride in her artwork, her knick-knacks, and her walls. They were a part of her environment that she could affect, and she kept the place neat. My wall art only made more work for her.

So I sat in the closet and colored, in darkness, on the walls.

I lay on my back on the floor and colored on the underside of the table on which lived several lush houseplants.

I squeezed against the wall and reached where only my little arms could reach and colored on the wall behind the dresser, on the wardrobe, the couch, the fish-tank.

(Decades later, while clearing their final dwelling of three lifetimes of treasure and crap, I wiped off the low standing white table where mom had dutifully raised her plants, and I turned it on it's side and became reacquainted with the scribbling and portraits of three year old me. Mostly red, but with a lot of purple and black, it was an indelibly

1

scribbled time capsule reminding me of the classified artist that needed to hide his gift as well as his feelings).

Dad often talked about "moving out" of the increasingly unpleasant and dangerous housing project where we lived. Apartments were being burglarized. People were getting mugged. Neighbors talked about the body of a teenage boy, found in the swamp across the street from our building.

In place of the nameless boy, I envisioned my own teen—my brother Kim—laying in the water, still and dead. Kim was ten and a half years my senior and I loved him with excessive abandon, waiting for the sound of him coming home from school so I could hug his thigh and step on his foot while he walked around the living room asking, "Where's Sethie? Has anyone seen Sethie?" Short lived as his affection was (he quickly tired of my kid-energy in favor of some teen-time behind one closed door or another), I always had something to look forward to. I thought of the dead boy and now some poor little brother may no longer have a Kim. I couldn't fathom how such ugly things could be.

I sensed that change would be good. "When are we moving?," I'd ask.

Dad would smile, "Soon."

And my excitement remained in check. I didn't yet know the reasons for my brother going away to school, for Dad going to the hospital, or for Mom having damp eyes during half of her waking hours, but I sensed that change would bring relief and so I asked all the time, lest they became distracted and forget that "moving" was a high priority.

Arrangements were finally made to relocate to another, better project called "Pomonok." It was in a part of northern Queens with the odd name, "Flushing"—which tickled me to no end.

The move was tough on Dad. I remember this period of time in feelings, not in vivid details, except for one.

On the day that we moved, the truck had left and Dad and I went around the apartment picking up and dust-brooming pennies, pencils, thumbtacks and dead water bugs that had hid in the "unders" and "behinds" of our stuff for many years. The unknown was not yet something that scared me, and I was riding the adventure taking us to our new town, our new apartment, my and Dad's wish fulfilled.

Dad came back into the empty apartment from the hallway after one last trash run and stood in the middle of the barren living room, hands on hips and scanning the place, taking it all in. I'd never been in a place as empty as this one, and I couldn't get my mind around the obvious truth that this was the same room that I knew so well, not bigger, just empty.

He looked at me and smiled. I smiled back and asked if we were going. He shook his head and from his pocket, produced a small box of crayons. He extended his arm down to hand them to me.

I took them and he squatted to meet my eyes. "One."

"One what?" I didn't understand the direction. One

crayon?... I wondered. Are we going to count now? Have I done something wrong?

He smiled bigger, held up an index finger and said, "Pick ONE wall."

Hawthorne, NY 1970 - age five

When I was five and he was fifteen, my brother Kim went away to school. "Reform school," I would sometimes hear it called. Unmanageable frictions between Kim and Dad led a social worker to recommend the school as a solution.

Dad's voice would raise first and Kim's would follow. Seconds later, Kim would be running down the long foyer toward our room, our father in pursuit. They fought constantly and Dad's temper was uncontrollable.

Through all this, I was sure my parents' difficulties had more to do with my sad demeanor than with my brother's coming of age.

The other boys at the residential institution were serial delinquents, criminals, drug offenders and psychiatric puzzles. My brother fell into the last category but quickly absorbed all manner of misbehavior from his fellow students and dorm-mates.

Kim came home with cool furniture he'd made in metal shop and scars on his fists. He made me proud and I could calculate no liability in my childish experience for his being away except that I missed him terribly. When the phone rang at dinnertime, I jumped up and down and asked if it was him calling. Mom handed me the phone, repeatedly reminding me that I only had a minute or two before he'd have to go. With him away, I essentially grew up an only child. Kim was my big buddy and, at the time, my hero.

We drove the hour plus up to White Plains where everyone seemed rich and white and onto the campus of Hawthorne, whose literature called it, "A residential treatment center for emotionally disturbed boys and girls." We walked across a vast lawn to where my brother bunked with other guys, other families visiting and quiet talks going on among the relaxed strollers. The place seemed ideal to me and I imagined his studies had come easy and his success would follow naturally. I was under the impression that my big brother was being allowed into an elite community of fortunates.

The first of the best friends he made at Hawthorne was Matt Bodenheim, grandson of Maxwell Bodenheim, a well-known and long ago murdered beat poet who newspapers had called "The King of Greenwich Village." Matt, too was a poet, with a mop of sandy hair and narrow, thoughtful eyes. I thought of Kim's friends as my big brothers, and I loved Matt the best. He was the first person whose intellect I was impressed with, very smart and even tempered, a trait with which I was unfamiliar. He listened patiently as I told him about school and the cartoons I was a fan of. My parents and I loved Matt and I became doubly excited when hearing that he would be coming home with Kim for a visit.

Another Hawthorne buddy—the first of two Erics— was portly and jovial and well liked by my mother. They sometimes came home together on extended weekends off from Hawthorne. Once when I wasn't getting the attention

I wanted from my brother and him, I kicked a hard shell guitar case that was sitting on my bed. It hit Eric in the face and he threw a fit. While I was at fault, it surprised my family and took some effort for my mother and Kim to calm him down. That was the only weird shit I ever witnessed coming from these lost boys who'd been shut away for their emotional shortfalls.

The second of the two Erics was a drummer, muscular and pot bellied with shaggy blonde hair. He remained a member of our family long after graduation from Hawthorne, living near us in Queens, eating over almost weekly, and eventually sharing an apartment with Kim—the last independent living situation my brother would enjoy. He was loud in general, and always laughed a *little* too loud and *far* too long. He once made a provocative joke, presumably to Kim, dad and me—the guys in the room—in front of mom. He laughed even harder when we all looked on in wonder, asking ourselves what the *fuck* was wrong with him. He embarrassed my family at Jewish holiday gatherings when other friends or relatives were visiting, unprepared for his crazies. I clearly remember one nice meal in progress, Eric making an insensitive comment, and the whole room going quiet. As a favor to him, I once typed up a letter of introduction to an adult film director as he dictated. He described himself as dedicated, hard working, and well hung. I made editorial recommendations, folded it up and he mailed it to the man he expected would change his life. I was fifteen. He never heard back and, if you asked him, he missed his boat.

Seth Branitz

As Kim's circle of influence began to extend to further reaches of drug culture—places Eric wanted nothing to do with—we saw less of him.

Once I became somewhat aware of Kim's challenges, I was surprised to hear that any of these boys had been delinquents. Just as I'd looked up to them when I was small, I would eventually follow their lead in my teens.

Kim moved into a halfway house on St. Marks Place and then to another they called "The Residence" in Rego Park. Run by an apparently sweet older couple named Mr. and Mrs. Vero, I was sad that they got to enjoy what seemed like a more harmonious dynamic with our Kim than we did. Kim would come home on weekends and other nights here and there. These visits were never without an outburst, my dad screaming or punching Kim, then threatening him and ultimately throwing him back out.

Once, when my dad was pushing on a bedroom door to get to my brother who was blocking it with his foot on the other side, Dad pushed the top of the door until it warped and then split. Another time, my brother (who had studied martial arts for years) responded to Dad's relentlessly swinging fists with a side kick. Dad fell to the floor, barely breathing and with several broken ribs.

The fighting between my brother and our dad was explosive and regular. The police were at our door many times, chatting with each of us, looking for signs of abuse, sitting my brother down for a talking to, always gentlemen and always the necessary de-fusers for a calmer family evening.

The Trouble With Kim

My father told my brother that he hated him, that he was no fucking good, to drop dead. Mom once told him that she wished she'd drowned him when he was a baby. There were always scowls and sarcasm, yelling in the streets and holes in doors.

A couple of years since we'd last been in touch, the second Eric began to call me now and then, to tell me how bad Kim looked and how worried he was about him. He said that Kim smelled bad and that he seemed high. When running into Kim, he'd try to encourage healthier behavior and asked him to hang out. He told me that we had to do something. "I know," I'd say. "He's my brother. I'm trying to help him."

I find it difficult to believe that these and other of my brothers' friends found their time at Hawthorne to be as befouled as he did. For him, he would eventually tell me, going there was punishment and he hated the entire time. He would continue throwing this misdeed in my parents' faces until the end. If, during an argument, Dad would threaten to throw him out, Kim would return with, "You already DID throw me out." He'd go on to say that he had been a child, that it was unfair, that it ruined his life, and that he'd never leave. These handy retorts left my parents depleted and out of ammunition.

My mother eventually told me what was, perhaps, an abridged version of the real reason that they'd sent Kim to Hawthorne. Dad had become crippled by his anger, unable to handle stress, and was coming undone. Kim's displays of adolescent rebellion, especially where they concerned paternal horn locking, were seen as a red flag by a social worker. He told my parents that the problem would just grow and that they'd be wise to remove the source. He made his recommendations and my parents followed up, followed through and, arguably, ruined their first son's life.

After my mother died, I found among a wad of letters, one that she had written to Kim and mailed to him at Hawthorne. In it she apologizes for subjecting him to the separation and says she missed him. She assures him that it's ultimately the best thing for everyone and says that they had to protect his brother, me. Even with ten years between us, apparently he was harming me in some way, and sending their fourteen year old boy away was the only way for them to deal with it.

I often blame. I find it challenging to attribute hardship and calamity to the simple wisdom of fate. I don't just accept those things that have gone before as unfortunate without wondering if maybe someone had done it a little differently, it could have worked out better. I loved my parents, but they fucked up.

Kim had a beautiful heart and a complicated but quick mind. He needed patience in a family that sought quick fixes. He needed space in a world that would give him none. He needed love but the store was closed.

I have no physical scars from that time period so I don't know if maybe he was being sadistic or if the alleged abuse was sexual in nature. I'm told that I experienced trauma but think my memory holds the incidents to which I can attribute most of that. I've undergone tons of therapy and thought hard on it and at this point I can't see any value in knowing one way or another.

His story is over and I'm just telling my version of it. Either way, I forgive him.

SUPERMAN, 1970 - AGE FIVE

RAYMOND WORE A white shirt, a black necktie and thick glasses. He smiled warmly and I trusted him. He reminded me of Clark Kent. We'd sit in a semicircle and although I didn't understand what the problems were, it seemed like my teen brother would shrink and dissolve into his chair under the glare of my father and the tearful gaze of my mom. I wonder if there was anything that I might have said in these family therapy sessions that led to the ultimate decision to send my brother to Hawthorne.

While he was away I would lay awake at night and stare at the big blank wall over my feet and imagine GOD. I'd heard mention of his name and never disputed his existence. I blindly trusted that he was a real entity that simply didn't bother with the likes of us. We were Jewish, and I hadn't seen artists renderings of the handsome, bearded man in Jesus' portraits, so as I'd stare up onto the wall, lit by the lampposts shining four stories below, GOD would appear in the softly smiling face of Raymond. I asked for nothing and he offered nothing except for assurance.

My family found answers—right or wrong—to tough questions while visiting with Raymond. I got comfort, and perhaps some misconception that therapists were certain kinds of fixers. That they heal and perform miracles FOR us.

For a few years while I was still small and my brother was away, I took two buses with my mom to an office at

Queens General Hospital to see Mrs. Weiner. She would ask questions as I colored with crayons, performed puppet shows for her, and built with blocks. I talked very little, if at all. Mom and I would have eggs, buttered toast and chocolate milk at the luncheonette by the bus stop before heading home. I don't think that my time with her hurt, but I doubt that it helped.

Stick, 1972 - AGE SEVEN

KIM ASKED DAD to foot the bill for the five hundred dollars he needed to buy his first car, a rusty, early 60s station wagon. Dad was concerned when he found out that the clunker had a standard transmission, but Kim told him that they'd taught him how to drive a stick at driver's-ed while at Hawthorne, when he was completing his high school years. It was a Valley Green Dodge with a smattering of rust about the fenders, cigarette burns and duct taped seats, and a green tennis ball perched atop the antenna. I loved it and was beyond proud of my brother. To me, the second family car meant that we were less poor.

When Dad completed the transaction and brought the car back to the project, we men took it out for a spin. My big brother was seventeen and I was seven.

I sat in her backseat and fastened the lap belt; glad to be there for my brother's landmark accomplishment.

At first I thought something must have been wrong with the car, as it revved loudly, suddenly jolted forward and then stalled. Dad firmly said "Easy off the clutch," and my brother tried again but each time he shifted, the car slammed forward and then stalled. Dad, fists clenched, began to yell about my brother not listening to him and then asked if he really had been taught how to drive on a car with a standard transmission. Kim screamed back that he had and while the bucking and yelling increased, we got nowhere.

The Trouble With Kim

We all knew that Dad could easily snap from his soft, depressive self into a rage with little or no provocation, leaving us speechless, especially in dealings with my brother. Attempts to neutralize fights between these two had been regular business at home. From as early as I can recall, I would take my brother's side and yell, "Leave him alone!," or some other command I'd heard from my mother in an earlier attempt to make the peace or rescue our underdog. Sometimes when I intervened, Dad would whip his head around and meet me with his crazy eyes and we'd pause. He'd either scream at me to get out of their way or he'd stomp off to his room, slamming the mirrored door behind him.

With Dad's impatience escalating, I demanded he stop yelling at Kim. Just as I did, the car came to a loud and violent stop, scaring me and throwing us all forward. Dad's right fist had been clenched for most of the several block voyage, but he now brought it to the side window and across the front seat where it connected to Kim's head with a crash. Kim reached to unlock the door but Dad grabbed his jacket and said, "Easy off the clutch, you son of a fuckin' bitch." Kim wouldn't give Dad the satisfaction of seeing him cry, grimaced in pain and resolved to continue the lesson. Knowing I was already in the way, I didn't even notice that I was crying until Dad glared at me and said, "I'll give you something to cry about." He barked directions and Kim failed again and again, until finally, he got the car rolling, slowing, turning, stopping, starting, getting on and off the Long Island expressway, parallel-parking and engaging the hand brake with relative smoothness and minimal talking back. Dad's scowl remained plastered on his face; Kim's wet, red and angry eyes spoke volumes. There was no resolution. There were no apologies.

As soon as we walked through the door, Mom knew things had gone wrong. We each retreated to our corners of the small apartment and suffered our respective disquiet in silence.

Dad took Kim driving a few more times and Kim would get good at driving a stick, but to this day I myself have not. I simply have no interest.

SELECT FAMILY HISTORY - 1973

MY FRATERNAL GRANDFATHER, Ben, had steely blue eyes and light hair and was know to friends as "Whitey." He died while my father was in the army. My dad told me that he'd had a brain tumor but I tend to believe my older cousin who told me that Whitey had fallen while drunk and died instantly when he hit his head on the sidewalk outside his bar, just one link in our family's chain of tragic addiction. My dad received an honorable discharge and came home. He bragged that his father, Whitey (who owned a driving school) had invented the mechanism that enabled a driving teacher in the passenger seat to ride the brakes from there in case a student was about to hit something he or she shouldn't. He never filed a patent or received any credit for his contribution to safe driving. I suppose it could be true, but I tend to doubt it.

He co-owned a bar with his brother in law, my great-uncle, Willy. Together—and eventually with the help of my grandmother—they ran a bookmaking business. He also owned the multi family house on Houston Street where my dad was born in a third floor bathtub. The building was eventually condemned by The City of New York in order to build a parking lot for a public school.

Dad told me many stories of regular encounters with Jewish Mafia figures such as Dutch Shultz and Bugsy Siegel. He said that they were always around, dressed sharp and that he never feared them. Over the years I've come to believe that my grandfather and Uncle Willy were, in some way, connected to the Jewish-Mob, and not simply with something as lowly as paying routine protection money or via the betting system involved in the boxing world. They enjoyed some relative privilege as a part of the uglier underworld that pervaded the already ugly tenement life of depression-era Lower East Side. This connection along with rental income from boarders in the house they owned kept them from suffering the worst of the depression, as my mother and her parents had in the Bronx.

Uncle Willie had been a welterweight contender for a time, fighting as Willie Harmon. For what could have been Willy's big break, the Mob had money on another fighter, the champ, and demanded that Willie throw the fight. Uncle Willy refused and they threatened to kill his whole family if he didn't. Dad described the scene after Willy threw the fight, Willy laying spread eagle on the mat, eyes wide open and staring into the flashing cameras.

There was another tale about how a guy on the street mouthed off to Willy only to find himself hanging on a hook by his coat against a brick wall. Dad loved retelling these stories of living vicariously through his uncle, his father, and mobsters during the first years of his life.

We drove to the cemetery in New Jersey when I was four to visit my father's father. They'd never mentioned that he was dead. I was excited. I'd only heard him mentioned a few times by then and liked my other grandfather very much, so I looked forward to meeting him.

While standing before a stone amid the shrubs and mounds, I asked Dad what the words and numbers said. He said his father's name and nothing more. I asked him where his father was. He pointed to an unkempt hedge standing taller than me and said that he was in there. I looked in but could make out neither a bed nor a body.

"What's he doing in THERE?!"

"Resting," he offered.

I was simultaneously disappointed and insulted. He must have known that we were coming!

My father and I would have many such incomplete conversations as the years went on. The subject of death was not one into which we would delve. Nor was sex.

Not until three decades later, just months before his death when his spirit was weak and his body breaking down, when he told Mom, my wife and me at the dinette table that he'd enjoyed the company of a prostitute in France during the war. I think we were all proud of him for cracking the armor just a bit. My mom rolled her eyes. Jenn and I laughed. Dad blushed and laughed along like a nine year old.

I've always told my sons that our ancestors, and all the people who came before us are not just faded black and white photos in some boring and irrelevant attempt to connect us to history. They were people, exactly like us. They felt sad, insecure, alone, hopeful, disappointed and needy. They were vain and they sought pleasure and avoided pain and were often completely self-conscious.

They loved puppies and sweets and got excited on holidays and when they saw rainbows. They picked their noses and their lives happened in the moment. They were alive. They were awesome. They may have been different, but they were just like us.

I wish I had known Whitey and Willy, their moms and their dads, and every animal they ever had as a pet. I wish I could spend a day with one of my great-great-grand mothers in Europe and I could learn about her struggles and light her up with the sight of her great-great-great-grandsons and make her laugh. I'd like to see the teenage faces of my ancestors. We'd discuss our collective and shared thousand-year-old issues over a bottle of bubbly water. I'd pay good money to hang with some 19th century relatives and demonstrate an electric guitar, let them hear Ray Charles and Fleetwood Mac, and show them how to use dental floss. I can imagine hearing our screams as we ride the Cyclone and feel our shared blood race through our veins as we watch Goodfellas meander through Grand Central Station looking up. I'd connect and relate and hang on every word. Blow them away. Be in awe.

I also wish my sons knew my mother, my father and my brother. Not just from pictures on the fridge and the many stories they listen to with hunger, but to understand, to engage, to touch.

I think a lot about what my life will have meant once I'm gone. It humbles, challenges and horrifies me in ways I can't even begin to talk about; but the most essential information I could hope to impart to the next generations, should such a duty come within my reach, is that I'm a person. That two hundred years from now, should any historical record of my existence persist, it will impart a sense of relating, of empathy, of awesome sameness.

I have no control over this, of course. I figure that the only way to guarantee a place in history is to invent something useful or to commit an atrocity on a grand scale. I'm not ambitious enough to do either.

What I can do is to keep on acknowledging the vitality of those who have passed. They were special, and they were ordinary. They tried hard and fell short. They lusted and they regretted. They invented and they threw fights. They worried and, hopefully, they got over it.

They died, but first they lived.

BLADE, 1972 - AGE SEVEN

AT LEAST ONCE a week, Dad sat at the end of the couch, one long leg over the other, watching the news. He shined his brown pocketknife against his yellowing t-shirt, and then dug his nail into the notch and unfolded the large blade. He held the tool wrapped under his index and middle finger, the sharp edge against the inside of his thumbnail. Slowly and gently he picked at the skin, lifting long peels off the hardened side of his thumb, exposing pink and red flesh. He took the blade in his other hand and proceeded to saw gently at the base of the newly freed skin. The cat sat to his right, eyes closed and purring. Dad wrapped his bleeding fingertip in short ribbons of Kleenex. The TV blared. No one gave it a second thought and I forgot about it for many years.

In my thirties, while reading about a depressed woman who would use a steak knife to trim any and all imperfections from the surface of her skin, I remembered Dad's wordless ritual. Until then, I'd never thought of these acts as one of the many symptoms of his craziness.

That's how living with him—with them—was. I didn't like it, but it was just the way life was. "Normal" for us was afraid, resentful and lacking. My days and nights were full of tension and tumult, but on occasion, I'd get a break, such as a tender moment on the couch with my father as he quietly ripped skin from his body.

Concussion, 1976 - AGE ELEVEN

I WAS VERY clumsy, but that didn't stop me from playing on the monkey bars, climbing trees, and using our mattresses and the couch as trampolines. On more than one occasion, I missed the mattress and ended up on the floor. I recall several times banging my head hard and then throwing up.

Of several concussions I suffered as a child, the most serious occurred on my eleventh birthday. I was regularly left alone by my parents to prepare for school from the time I was in second grade. I wore the apartment key on a shoelace hanging from my neck. This was common among my friends.

I toasted an English muffin, buried the nooks and crannies under butter and jelly, dropped it jelly side down on the green carpet in the living room, and tried in vain to clean up the mess.

My mom would surely freak out when she saw the discolored carpet later that day, but I let my fear of the impending consequences rest as I walked the two blocks through the project. It was April 29th and the spring sun was shining. The walkways between our network of seven story buildings were bustling. For no particular reason, I felt good.

I'm told that what happened next is that I engaged in a pre-schoolbell game of ringalivio—a higher energy tag game with teams—and a husky kid named Chris Berman and I ran full speed around a paddle-ball wall toward one another and met with a crash, his head or shoulder into my abdomen. My kidney and some ribs were badly injured and I went over his shoulder and landed on my head.

My poor mom got a call from the principal and she came to my unconscious side. She rode with me in the ambulance to Booth Memorial Hospital. I have only a few snapshot memories of my hospitalization. They all involve doctors quizzing me. A few weeks are lost to amnesia, and neighbors and friends got a kick out of asking if I recalled their hospital visits. I didn't, and in some case doubted the validity of their stories.

Headaches and blurry vision led to a prescription for glasses. They only made the headaches worse, though, and I stopped wearing them. Within a few years my eyesight improved and the headaches subsided.

Prior to the accident, I was doing very well in school, performing at or above my grade level. After returning to school, however, it took me a very long time to read short passages and my comprehension of math became an object of great frustration for my parents and myself. Terms like dyslexia and hyperkinetic impulse disorder were thrown around, but no solutions. I never found my educational footing again.

I waited for Mom to chew me out for my part in the red stain on the carpet but it never happened.

When I returned to school over a month later I was told that Chris (the big kid) was scared that I was "going to kick his ass." The poor guy had enough trouble with the guilt of nearly killing me. I felt bad that he was worried, and the thought of holding him responsible had never entered my mind.

When we finally crossed paths in the hallway, I said, "Hi Chris," he said "Hi," we both smiled and never spoke again.

Clouds, 1975 - age ten

THE CLOUDS I grew up with were deep fire pink, candy purple, and red. They were blue and brown, friendly and fascinating. Sometimes, at dusk, I sat at the window watching the dark clouds against the light sky change to lighter clouds against the dark. They swept across the city skyline in slices and puffs, feathers and strokes.

The smokestacks and car emissions, we're told, provided the particles—carbon mostly—that created our pinks, blues and oranges; some of the most dramatic sunsets on the planet and the finest ones I've seen—I had only to tilt my head away from my sketchpad, through the west-facing window in my room, toward the near heavens to witness creation, animated and immense, infinite and right fucking there.

I tuned in nightly to watch the cityscape go from dreary grey and black to silhouettes before gorgeous technicolor and candy. The deeper the colors, the darker the bricks, I devoured my sky like an enthralling movie, knowing there were precious few minutes before it would end, wishing it could go on. I longed to live there but knew that whatever the day brought, it's end would interrupt nature's vast rainbow dance, that for all it's healing majesty, a problem was stirring, maybe even in the next room, and the darkness was just moments away.

Bat-shit and Jewel, 1976 - age eleven

My dad always walked to Jewel Pharmacy for advertised two-for-one deals on shower curtains and other shit merchandise we didn't really need (we only had one shower), and protested loudly if told that the thing had sold out. The girls at checkout were afraid of him.

Once a gal rang him up for a sixteen pack of toilet paper and he said that she got the price wrong. When she calmly told him that his price was for the twelve-pack, he took it in both hands, tossed it halfway across the store and took out his cash to pay as if the transaction was proceeding smoothly.

He brought me along too. I was also the one to go with him to the community center when government distributions took place. He came home with the bubbie-cart filled with logs of processed government cheese, butter and powdered milk. When I was little, I thought it a good deal; free food, and time with my dad. As I grew, though, so did my shame and I was horrified to think that anyone would know that we were so poor or that we were connected, my father and me.

My relationship with my father was very different from the one Kim had with him. They fought and Kim felt the need to prove himself. He craved approval and vindication. I mostly saw Dad as a victim, a sad and unusual guy, and eventually, as a bit of a spectacle in our community

27

what with his baggy pants nearly falling off, his childish confrontations with merchants and rental office staff, and his ever worsening cars. I vacillated between feeling protective of, and embarrassed by, my dad.

Even other kids in the project called us poor. I don't know if their situation was any more fortunate than ours, but as soon as I heard the words, "your family is on welfare," from a dirtbag neighbor kid named Jeff Ross when I was nine, I began to hold Dad in contempt and to wish I had a different family. I was more disappointed in him than angry. I wanted to live with another family and began to notice how rich people lived on TV and in movies. I thought about having a nice house of my own like the Bunker's, or a sprawling Manhattan flat like The Jefferson's. Mom would have loved that. I noticed that families were capable of confronting challenges with grace and with fun, as on The Brady Bunch, and that even where lower social status was a central theme, such as on Good Times, there was no lingering crisis, darkness nor deficit of love or support.

We were fucked up, and I knew that, which meant that I was fucked up.

4-C, DECEMBER, 1977 - AGE TWELVE

THE STRINES WERE an Irish Catholic family of five who lived at the other end of the hall, literally twelve steps away. The kids were pale, with ruddy cheeks and shiny black hair. They looked like their dad, Harold, an overweight union dockworker with a large bald spot always shining beneath his long combover. The mom, Nettie, was gangly and redheaded, and had a short fuse with her family, but never with me. It was in her presence that I first understood what it meant for a person to "bite someone's head off."

Russell was a year younger than I, and Tracy a year older. Beautiful Holly was a few years older and the first object of my desire. Once, when being called over to play while their parents were out for the evening, Holly was comfortable walking about in her panties and a bra. It was a long while before I could get that image out of my head.

We three younger kids spent a large chunk of our childhoods in each other's apartments or in the hallway hanging out together. We spent so much time that sibling-like spats inevitably became common. Russell was a terrible loser at board games and I wasn't willing to lie and tell him that he'd won —as his sibs were known to do—just to keep him happy. Tracy and I would disagree about what channel to watch or over shallow facts about people we both knew, but we'd get over it, come knocking, and rejoin forces in defiance of boredom.

Seth Branitz

The narrow hallway was dim and bleak and we'd sit on the brown and tan tiled floor and talk for hours, play Rummy or Go-Fish, or run and slide in our socks. We'd sometimes retreat to the stairway, where we could engage in talks of questionable decency, slide down using our asses as sleds and employ the natural and long reverb with ghost noises, screams and songs. I raced down and up those stairs multiple times each day for more than a decade and it was there, my voice adorned with a city-block of natural reverb, that I first fancied myself a singer.

Many of our evenings were spent in one of our apartments, in pajamas, playing games or watching television until we got tired of one another or a parent came to remind us that it was a school night.

I was much closer to Tracy. She and I shared an unending love of TV and of music. We understood each other. We sang pop hits and songs from A Chorus Line together and acted out scenes and homemade comedy skits.

One involved me standing behind her with my hands sticking under her arms, hers behind her back. She'd speak and I'd spontaneously gesture, waving my hands and pointing around. It was great fun and we seemed to share an uncanny synchronization. While putting on a show for my mother, I didn't realize that I kept on touching her quickly evolving, twelve year old chest and the extreme expressions on her face, trying to remain in character but considering a new boundary, made my mom pee in her pants. I had no idea what was so funny until Mom explained it to me later that night when she laughed so hard that she again had to excuse herself. I was embarrassed and delighted all at the same time, and clumsily apologized to Tracy the next day when we both had a good laugh as well, a burgeoning lust apparent to both of us. A short time later, and in a purely experimental spirit, she allowed me a proper feel.

They went to St. Nicholas of Tolentine Catholic School receiving what I assumed was a higher quality education than us public school kids. I didn't know from church bazaars, big fun holidays, or the giving or getting of multiple gifts for any reason whatsoever. They wore uniforms and I thought this evidence of how serious and superior their education must have been. They looked like little businessmen and ladies in contrast to the second-hand hippies and food-stamp vagabonds attending P.S. 201.

For several years I shared in the Strine Christmas rituals of putting up the plastic tree and decorating it. One year, Russell won a kitten at a church event. We'd just placed a round of ornaments on the tree when little Mikey came dashing through the living room, leapt half way up, scampered and clawed his way to the top, bringing the whole thing crashing down. A concern for Mikey's well being notwithstanding—and remembering that this predates the Internet—this was the coolest thing I'd ever witnessed.

When the tree was complete I made my way back across the hall, the flashing lights, vibrant bickering and festive music muting to a dreamy quiet as soon as their front door closed, and brace myself for the disappointing constant of my own two-bedroom apartment. I entered to the dimly lit relative vacancy and walked to the couch where Dad was watching a war documentary while picking at his cuticles and smoking cigarettes. He patted his thigh as an invitation to lay my head there and I did.

Our electric menorah sat in the window, plugged into an extension cord and humbly exclaiming among the thousands of project windows, most adorned with colorful Christmas lights or through which we could see many a well-loved tree, that 'here lives a Jew.' Looking out the window during this season there were Jesus loving folks for as far as the eye could see. In their midst I felt an odd, non religious kinship with the occasional windows in which there shone the orange or blue bulbs of a menorah. To me, these weak beacons seemed to unite us in the sad exclusion to which we were banished and expressed neither the celebration nor the privilege that the bolder, brighter and more festive lights did for these other, more fortunate households. The evidence was clear. We were the others. They were the chosen ones.

One year my father, perhaps detecting my sense of deprivation, perhaps his own, brought home a small evergreen plant and declared it a Hanukkah bush. I loved this idea and with my parent's permission and a particular skill for decorating as I'd done my time interning with the Strines, I began to adorn the sorry array of twigs and needles with ribbon-cut glossy magazine pages, pulled strips of cotton balls and jewels of rolled up aluminum foil. I felt proud.

The bell rang and Mom answered the door. When

Tracy walked in, spotted our project, and smiled. I lost any ambition for having it become a ritual. While her smile might have indicated admiration, I read it as pity and all I could think about was the failure before me, how I should have just acted satisfied with my other-ness, and how, once again, I wished I wasn't a Jew.

My father's birthday was December 23rd and I once asked him if he ever felt cheated by having a birthday so close to Christmas and Hanukkah, as I'd heard was the case with some kids of my generation. He didn't seem to understand the question. For him, neither fuss nor gifts were ever an expected part of either date.

On Christmas Eve I stayed up late and squatted by my bedroom window. Looking northwest I could see straight to the city and up to the flight paths of passenger jets, always one light just coming into view, always the brightest disappearing on the horizon as it pulled down to the runways at JFK. Various other aircraft were approaching or leaving La Guardia, Newark or one of the smaller airports in Westchester or on Long Island. I watched for a cluster, lower to the ground, possibly with a red light at the lead. Tracy and Russell were asleep and would miss Santa, but I would get a good look long at the fat fucker, even if his sled bore nothing for me.

I awoke on Christmas glad for the time off from school and watched morning television shows with Mom in the dinette. We compromised by switching between Dinah Shore and Captain Kangaroo. Mom and I made toasted English muffins and cottage cheese drizzled with maraschino cherry juice. Although there would be no presents for me, and I would have received only one for Hanukkah (our eight-night ritual was limited to the twist of the bulb in the electric menorah, no prayer, no stated gratitude, no gift), I felt a guilty warmth when hearing the TV people report on Christmas delicacies, festivities and traditions. I loved Rudolph. I was mesmerized by the Yule Log. They all seemed to make the world a happier place. It was no ones fault that I was born to the wrong religion.

After a while I'd go to the Strines and sit by as they deconstructed their towers of treasure. I'd be welcome to help tear the wrapping paper off of select packages and would take charge of crumpling it up into tight balls and stuffing them into trash bags for a neater experience in the overcrowded living room. This was my contribution to their Christmas.

I'd touch, try and play with anything I chose and would sit in on the maiden round of whatever new board game that Santa had brought. I'd help put double-D batteries in Russell's new this and tell Tracy how nice she looked in her pretty new that. I'd eat cookies and drink hot chocolate and smile and laugh and simultaneously love my friends and recoil in envy.

I wonder what it must have been like for them. I think they felt sorry for me. They knew I was poorer than they and that my family had unique problems. How strange it must have been for their parents. This most sacred ritual, reinforcing their faith and cherishing their family by spending time in pajamas and adorning them with all manner of material distraction, and here's this pathetic little neighbor kid crashing the party. Maybe they felt trapped by my presence; too neighborly to let my parents know that Christmas morning really was a private affair. Maybe there was a sense of duty in allowing me a glance of how their god rolls. To grant me a feel for how the other 999 out of 1,000 lives. Then when they thought it was enough, they'd send me back to my dark home across the hall. I wonder if they'd ever talked it over with my parents to establish boundaries, decide on a time limit. Maybe it was a controlled experiment drawn up and carried out by a bi-partisan committee. Or if they just played it by ear, allowing it until they thought enough was enough. Thanks for visiting. Time to go. Run along. There's nothing more for you here, little Jewish boy.

Or was it just as confusing and tolerated by all parties? I bet. The kids all just considered it hanging out. Both sets of parents were probably respectively embarrassed, speechless for fear of offending the other.

Discovering that there is a Hanukkah of celebration, joy and gifts has somewhat narrowed the divide between "us" and "them" for me, although I've only dabbled.

We grew apart in our teens, the Strine kids and me. I moved out and never saw them again.

I'd like to thank them for including me in their joy and in their privilege. But even more, I wish I had the opportunity to let our parents know that, faced with the choice of either being tempted and teased by all the excellent things I would never have, or to remain safe in the isolation of our joyless home, they made the better choice.

I liked seeing my friends happy.

Beams, 1977 - age twelve

On a sunny morning, lying in the bedroom I shared, part time, with my brother for most of twenty-one years, the sunlight that snuck past the tattered and yellowed window shade made the best of the dust in the air to demonstrate itself in glorious, spectral beams. I looked on in relaxed contentment as the thick light (mostly dead skin cells, I'm told), swirled like water over and through itself. Heaven extended a hand. Thought was unnecessary. It was splendid. I was as patient and as weightless as the magic specks.

There was nothing I needed.

There was nothing I owed.

There was no one I feared.

There was nothing I regretted.

There was nothing to aspire to.

There was nowhere to be.

I was this dust and was this light.

There was nothing wrong.

... with me.

A few years later I saw these beams again, but now they had weight; and I only watched for a while because the world was crumbling and there was somewhere else I needed to be.

RED, 1978 - AGE THIRTEEN

MARYANNE COGLIN was a Raggedy Ann doll. Orange hair, freckles, tall, lanky and project-poor, she wore holey overalls and dirty tank tops and was always rushing off to somewhere.

I used to stare at her when I knew she wouldn't catch me. Her beauty was the first I recognized to be understated, effortless and intense. She was androgynous, aloof and cool. Oblivious to the routine we kids endured without question (school, playground, shopping with our parents), Maryanne Coglin shuffled to the beat of her own psychedelic drum. She'd pass through these activities of ours from time to time, rushing and intense, and I think we all kind of silently agreed that while she was harmless, her presence made us uneasy.

She disappeared for months at a time and then reappeared with some striking new development—grew a foot, cut off all her hair, arm in a sling, scars, cigarettes, zits, tits; she was a mystery and a bit of a neighborhood celebrity. Some said that she spent time in Creedmoor, the psychiatric hospital that loomed on the skyline to the east. Someone else said that she was locked up in juvie. We all grew quiet when she passed, several theories always circulating on what new trouble had most recently befallen her.

I was flicking bottle tops into chalk drawn squares on the sidewalk outside my building—a game called scully—

one afternoon in sixth grade; Maryanne, long legged and barefoot, came striding through with a large brown paper bag. She called, "Who wants hits?" and several of the older kids left their station and skipped into line behind her as they disappeared down the path headed to the schoolyard.

By then I was aware of the smell of pot, the color of Valium and the taste of beer, but had not partaken beyond a curiosity that bordered on ambition. This was the first time I'd heard the term, "hits," but instinctively knew it's meaning.

I would have liked to get high with Maryanne, to have her attention, and to have done more, but it was not to be. The only specific exchange I ever clearly remember us having was in Junior High when at the beginning of one fall day, an odd sight appeared on the stairs next to me as I headed to homeroom. This was the only time I ever remember seeing her in school.

I said, "You're here!"

She smiled beautifully. "Yeah … gonna give it a try."

I wished her luck, she received it, and we both meant it. I looked for her the next day and for weeks after that. She never returned.

Seasons would pass with no sign of Maryanne until she'd show up, concerned, intense, messed up. She grew into a very tall young woman, bones rippling in her back, scabs on her freckled face, clothes dirty and sometimes hanging off of her, revealing body parts that had once intrigued me, but which now worried and repulsed me. It would be a while before I would become intimate with addiction. The arc of her descent was the first one I witnessed.

My father had a long hospitalization when I was in high school and although I was asked to merely move his car some mornings before school to honor the alternate side of the street parking signs, I instead drove Dad's car to and from school in Jamaica each day, except when I cut class.

Headed home one afternoon, I slowed to make a right turn onto Parsons Blvd, a tree lined row of apartment buildings and parallel parking, when Maryanne strode from between parked cars right toward my passenger side door. I slowed down and she bent to look into the car. When our eyes met, we both froze; she quickly turned away and walked. I resumed my drive up the street and in my rear view mirror I saw her approach the next car in her very short denim shorts and tube top. She leaned in the passenger window for a few seconds, and got in. I was nauseous with protective disbelief and some sort of displaced shame.

Rumors were all we had of Maryanne, and while we were children they bounced between flattering and cruel. Once we became young adults they were upsetting. Before we were grown, they ceased. The last one I heard was that Maryanne, like so many other phantoms and friends, had died of AIDS.

My childhood is a junkyard of sparse associations with rusty personalities; filled with things I wish hadn't happened and others I wish I'd noticed or engaged. I have a great fondness for many of my neighbors and friends and a gnawing contempt for others.

Then there are the ghosts—faces I'd known for years but about whom I never learned a thing, only assumptions and biases—exorcised from a safe distance. Any shift in the stars might have influenced our encounter, which might have ignited a conflict or a friendship.

Maryanne appeared and disappeared, mysterious and impressive, until she entered the next plane, an eternally adolescent, freckled and fucked up legend. I hope that there was some richness and comfort amid her dysfunction and alienation. I'm glad, at least, that unlike so many other ghosts, she and I shared kindness at least once, though I wish there were more.

Magazines, 1978 - age thirteen

As a child, while sitting in any number of waiting rooms with my mother, she came to a point in the sitting when she adjusted her posture, looked around the room and began to hum.

The magazine on her lap remained open, slid up to her belly, and the humming got louder and busier and she coughed. She began an idle conversation with me, speaking a little more loudly than usual and when I answered, she responded to the answer in a very over-appreciative manner.

"Is that *right*, Seth? You had a *spelling* test today? And how did you *do?*"

At the loudest, most humm-full and cough-ous moments I could just make out the faintest sound of tearing paper. Then she reiterated the substance of the talk—of which there was none—and continued to subtly squirm as she folded and tucked her secret into her treasure chest pocketbook.

Eventually we were called to the desk for a receipt, and then headed out on our merry way. Later, I asked her what the magazine thing was all about. She smirked for a few seconds, looked around as if to be sure we were alone, and then told me about her prize with erupting excitement:

> A recipe at the rental office,
> … an interview at social security,
> … a book reviews at the podiatrist,

… a short story at the shrink.

Her charade was a regular occurrence and I had no judgment on her choice to tear articles from magazines. I loved her, and if she wanted it, she should have it. For a long time I didn't even think that it was a form of stealing. I hadn't even considered a possible, less sneaky alternative until I was much older. "Why don't you just ask them if you can have it?" She said that they were "office property," and that they wouldn't like that very much. Perhaps she was afraid that they might have said no. *Maybe she liked the rush.*

At home, Mom had folders of glossy color pages with one or two rough edges where the documents had been torn from their host, including family recipes from Good Housekeeping, sound advice from Ladies Home Journal, candid interviews from Redbook, quizzes from Cosmo, and models from McCall's. She had piles of faces and scenes she hoped to eventually get around to reproducing in a painting or a sketch. She hung adorable animals on the fridge. She made collages.

Magazines were a luxury for her and she only occasionally purchased one at the supermarket checkout. When she did, she dove in, rekindling the now-dormant intellectual and tabloid-privy delight of her school years. She sat up straight; legs crossed, with a cold beverage in a tall, sweaty glass, and was momentarily in the know.

To me, the recipes were uninteresting, the articles too long and the pictures – ordinary. I eventually found fault with the lion's-share of my family's behavior and I thought that stealing pages was just a symptom of my mothers' oddness. The prospect of anyone finding out that she was part thief, part vandal would just add to the disgrace of our eccentricity—being on welfare, Dad being unemployable, us having the oldest, crappiest car in the project, and so on. The magazine clippings were part of a major clutter factor at home, piles and folders sitting on top of her dresser and in an old canvas bag at the bottom of her wardrobe.

When my brother took me to one of the two supermarkets within walking distance of our apartment, he skillfully smashed one pound Hershey bars and twelve-packs of gum down his pants, headed for the door and then we ran. My own solo debut was at Wainright's, the local family-owned department store where I tucked a balsa wood airplane into my sock. A couple of my friends were giggling with admiration when I heard a woman's voice ask, "You wanna go to jail?" She stood over me, eight feet tall, hands on hips and head cocked sideways, her huge square frames floating over her enormous eyes and I was terrified. She repeated the question and I said no, that I was not really going to take it, only showing my friends how to carry it. She cocked her head even further (I don't know how it remained attached to her neck), said to put the toy back on the shelf and to get out. I complied and the gang followed me out the back door. They began shrieking with nervous energy and I walked faster, staying in front so they wouldn't see my eyes pooling with tears. Within a few years there were photos of me on the shoplifter corkboards in the offices of several supermarkets in and around my neighborhood. I still like to think that I was good at it, but I suppose that—just as with school—I didn't apply myself.

I knew what stealing was and I knew what lying was. I knew that people who were in jail were often good people who had done something wrong. I was a good boy when I stole cash from my dad's pockets so I could buy candy and ice cream and then pot and mescaline and I cheated friends out of drugs we were supposed to share, taking the larger half or "stepping on" *(diluting)* their portion if I had time alone with it. I still thought I was a good person when a pothead teacher I knew lived in a basement apartment on my girlfriends block and I regularly snuck in above the doorway to raid her stash or grab handfuls of "roaches" that filled her impressive collection in a large, glass bowl. I pretended it was OK to rip off employers, taking food and cleaning products and money and machines and hours and more. I thought I was justified when walking out of Bloomingdale's and Filene's Basement with several layers of clothes under the baggy ones I'd worn walking in with, security sensors crudely liberated with the scissors I'd brought along. The stores wouldn't miss the stuff. I'm not hurting anyone. I'm still a good guy. *Fuck them!* I attacked, robbed, dealt, cheated and justified my way through adolescence and well into my twenties.

Then, when I stopped getting high, I began to obsess on all these more harmless aspects of my deviant past; the lying and dealing, and stealing, and a lot of other petty crap. I remember new ones all the time and while I made a firm commitment to be truthful and take nothing that didn't belong to me, this didn't quell the feeling that I'd spoiled the good person I used to be. I even had a job telemarketing merchandise that I knew was overpriced, and while I hated doing it, I stayed too long. I hated myself for having been a fuckhead and for putting my own, momentary desires before the happiness of others. I vowed to be honest and helpful, and to pay back anyone who I could.

In this regard I've thus far done an imperfect job, but I keep trying.

I reflect on my progress *(or lack thereof)* regularly and do five-year check-ins: Am I more truthful? More helpful? Less of a dick? I've been on a pretty good run of affirmative responses to all of these, with the possible exception of the last, which is entirely subjective.

Basically, it's about doing what's right. Right? It's about defining the lines, retracing them with thick marker so that they are not easy to blur and so that I can't kid myself about what's ok and what's not. So at present, if it's not mine I don't take it.

With one exception. I steal magazines. It's not a case of my evil inclination winning over my goodness. It's a clear choice, one with which I'm quite OK. In the occasional office magazine library, I hone in. I imagine looking up at my mother with a knowing, clandestine glance—two generations of notorious Queens paper thieves about to do a "job." We look left and we look right. She gives the signal and I pull it flat to my belly, look around, smiling in case a distraction is needed, and hum loudly as I pull the pages from the spine. Or I just walk around with the whole magazine. Exchanging information, asking if we expect rain, taking care of business, holding the thing right under their noses, offering them the chance to stop me. But they never do.

I'm giving you a chance here! I have something that belongs to you! I didn't walk in with this, but I'm about to walk out with it! But they're lost in my cunning charade. And I make my next appointment, take my invoice, documentation or prescription, and head for the door.

I walk at my usual pace, but my heart is dancing and my mind is running down the block, chocolate cracking against my groin and my dead mother skipping next to me, alive and victorious.

Outside, 1978 - age thirteen

There was a summer when I was a boy—a whole summer and well into the school year when I would not go outside without my mother, father, my brother or my grandmother. I'd been teased by what seemed like a cross-section of the young population and bullied by a certain few mutant assholes and it looked like this was not going to stop.

A group of older boys had pummeled me with hardened snowballs and when I fell to the ground and took cover they continued, standing over me and pitching full speed at my head.

A fat kid named Jonathan Horney had sat on me, slowly squeezed his fat fingers around my neck, crushing and choking me out. He got up laughing and waddled off to catch up with his friends.

While waiting on line at Steve, the ice cream man's little red, white and blue truck, I could expect to have my ears flicked or my neck slapped with a leatherette bus pass holder.

I was called Jew, fag, poor and more; a common threat during school hours was, "Your ass is grass at three."

It happened at random times and when it wasn't supposed to. I received a neck-cracking blow to the side of my head while shooting baskets when a troubled boy wailed the ball at me from five feet away. I watched dead-eyed John Hallahan swing a baseball bat within inches of the head of a disabled boy named Khan (a strange, scrawny, hyperactive kid whose eyes appeared freakishly large through his inch-thick lenses).

I began to wake up expecting that today would be the day that someone would hit me with a stick, stab me with a pocket knife, or push me down the stairs. I was in the habit of turning around to see if anyone was walking behind me, hiding in the bushes or waiting in the elevator. I sometimes waited outside my building for an adult to walk up so that I wouldn't have to enter the lobby or ride the elevator alone. If I couldn't wait, I'd yell up to our fourth floor window and ask Mom or Dad to come down for me.

Life was frightening, but turned dark when my mother told me of John Cavalo's last ride. He lived in the apartment right below ours and he was seventeen and one of the boys I looked up to. When I learned that he'd driven halfway across the Verrazano Bridge, gotten out and left his Pro-Keds where he jumped, I was numb. Here was someone who appeared to be happy, popular and confident. Someone whom I sought to be like. Was I going to be like him? I feel the resignation even now as I recall it.

We lived in the building where the housing police had their headquarters and we'd see them and hear their radios, their sirens, and their squeaky brakes all day and night from our fourth floor window. At the same time I was learning from my older brother that the police were evil and that they made trouble for harmless young people and that they were "pigs." George Harrison even wrote one of my favorite songs about just this. I watched the officers come and go as I hummed the melody and repeated, "Have you seen the little piggies crawling in the dirt?"

And on a recent spring afternoon walking in Alphabet City with my brother, we were approached by a cop who asked my brother if he had a problem. When my startled teen-aged brother (skin tanned and curly hair closely cropped) failed to answer, the cop said, "No speakee English, Spic?" I never again looked at officers Carmine or Eddie without a measure of contempt. I was frightened of our protectors. And my own protectors, my parents, were quickly melting off of their traditional pedestals as their own eccentricities, failures and neuroses became increasingly apparent to me.

Childhood brought a gradual discovery that the world was an unsafe place. It was a threatening and relentless gauntlet of shame and disappointment through which I had no chance of battling.

My dad was not effective at recognizing or talking me through problems, exerting discipline, or at inspiring me. His remedy for my shade of summertime blue was to threaten me with signing me up for basketball at the Flushing Y. I screamed that I wouldn't go and he screamed louder and, thankfully, it never happened. I'm sure that he thought that the sport that left him with many fond teen imprints was going to deliver me to a similarly cheery boyhood memory. But skinny and uncoordinated, I never played sports, so this magic bullet scheme of his would have ensured certain failure. I was totally disinterested in the prospect, as well as by the thought of any social interaction beyond the walls of our two-bedroom Pomonok apartment. Now on top of the fear and isolation, I felt that I had failed my dad and my situation grew dimmer.

The world was full of muggers, rapists, gangs, Nazis, bikers and Son of Sam, so I stayed in the house. I stayed by myself or with my immediate family. I drew and wrote and played guitar and watched TV and did projects with my mom and I slept. I tried to seem OK although I was growing more deeply depressed and I made myself look busy, lest my dad bring up the Y again or feel guilty over not showing up for me in the ways a needy son needs a father. He couldn't. And for the first time, but far from the last, I felt trapped. I didn't understand that these were fears and concerns and perceptions and issues. I thought they were facts. I didn't think that anyone, anywhere could ever have gone through this before and the thought never occurred to me that I could talk with someone about it or that it might end.

Sometime during the second fall, having fielded crowds while traveling through school without incident and feeling perhaps a little less trapped, I responded to my mom's suggestion that I go to the market for her with a timid but bright, "OK." She was pleased and that prepared me even more for my lone trek into the suddenly safer outside world. The sun was shining and I exchanged waves with a few kids, out with their mothers or playing ball. When I got to Jewel Avenue I heeded the traffic signal, waiting for the illuminated *"walk"* signal (even though there were no cars in sight and others had begun walking), then I pushed the wobbly bubbie-cart across the street feeling the way I thought an adult might feel.

The Trouble With Kim

I was a little giddy over this foreign and groundless joy. I can do this, I thought. Even as I pondered my regret over missing so many afternoons cooped up in my dark, dusty room, I was OK.

The Boulevard curved toward the supermarket. A few storefronts before its' entrance, a couple of tall, menacing teenage boys, one holding a stickball bat, turned out from behind a wall and stood right in front of my wagon. "Shopping for mommy?" one of them mocked. I froze, knowing I couldn't outrun them with the cart and not willing to give it to them. "Give us your money, faggot." One pulled a knife from a sheath tucked into the front of his pants. The streets seemed suddenly deserted and I was helpless to protest, but I rolled my cart back a foot or two then shoved it into the knife wielder's legs. They pushed me against the glass storefront, punched me repeatedly in the head and stomach and emptied my pockets. As I wiped my tears on the walk home, rolling the cart with no groceries, I hoped that the one guy would put his knife back down his pants in a hurry and cut his dick off. I hoped that they'd both get hit by a bus and spend their lives regretting how they'd spent their last five minutes of able-bodied sadism.

During the thousands of times I've replayed this walk in my mind, I've sometimes waded in the terror and disappointment. Others, though, have played out an alternate ending involving a spinning back kick that sent one through the plate glass window, that hot girl, Linda Rivera watching from the curb and falling instantly in love with my courage and ability. Other times, I grabbed their ears and cracked their heads together, both of them falling to the ground unconscious, Three Stooges style.

I didn't tell my parents about the knife. I didn't want to make a bigger deal out if it than it already was, and somehow I feared that they would now want me to stay home. This surprised even me, but whatever transpired, I was done being inside. My parents and therapist feared that this would set me back as long stints of agoraphobic isolation are not usually bookended by a bully and a mugging.

I reclaimed my place as an outsider, but on these streets and in these parks. The fresh air and variable stimulation didn't grow my self-worth or make me a better citizen, but whatever self-defeating strategies I was inclined to conjure, I now did it outside.

I encountered one of the mugger kids a couple of months later. He was shopping with his mother, saw me and then avoided eye contact. I lingered close to where they were and spent a few minutes trailing them from aisle to aisle. I had no plan, but knew that he knew who I was and enjoyed reminding him of his wrongdoing. I didn't have the courage to confront him but I calmly taunted the fucker while he shopped with his mommy.

I recently took my sons with me back to the project for a sort of reunion I'd read about on Facebook. Most of the people I'd grown up with and around had moved. The place is huge and many people have lived there during the half-century since I arrived, but I had a feeling that I might see someone I needed to see.

Ritchie Brown was there and I was thrilled to see him and to introduce him to my boys. Ritchie is a developmentally disabled guy a couple of years older than I am. He was always around, slid in and out of everyone's crowd and seemed more or less protected by the community at large, white and black alike. He used to remember everyone's birthday and his deep voice never wavered from a monotone singsong drone. He shook each of my sons hands and repeated their names several dozen times, making them smile, which made him smile, and renewed my affection for him and his strange ways.

He asked how my parents were and where my brother lives. I told him of their respective untimely demises and he nodded at me and said, "OK, Seff." After a few short exchanges, some time with Ritchie, and a couple of stories, we left. I'd gotten what I'd come for.

As we walked back to our car, my sons held my hands tightly and asked what it was like growing up there, a place so different than the upstate suburb they call home.

I told them that the whole trip was worth it because I'd had some time with Ritchie.

In unison, they said, "He's nice."

KINDLING, 1979 - AGE FOURTEEN

WHEN STAYING AWAY from home was most important to me, I found myself starving for attention. I didn't actually choose friends; rather I assimilated into a crowd of boys who didn't tell me to leave. They were all a year or more older than me, and had more in common with one another than I did with any of them. A group of para-militaristic rejects whose pastimes included running around in the woods with machetes, throwing now-rotten eggs that they'd stolen by the case from the loading dock at the supermarket, and talking obsessively about war and weapons, they didn't want me there, but there I was.

I went with them to see *Apocalypse Now* at the Midway Theatre on Queens Boulevard and they hooted and cheered whenever something crude or violent was said or done on that big screen. I, on the other hand, became mortified and depressed. I sunk lower and lower into my seat, eventually closing my eyes and wishing for it to be over, hoping that none of them would notice me being small and weak. (I had the same traumatic reaction when seeing Pink Floyd's, *The Wall.*)

Depictions of suffering and violence such as displayed in the film were very hard on my senses. I tend to hyper empathize and instead of bearing witness, I embody the suffering itself. Slaves in *Roots,* tourists in *The Poseidon Adventure,* precious, misunderstood Kong being shot down and falling long from the sky, poor Sophie and the one she choose not to choose; they are me and I am them and I'm learning that there are certain things that I just shouldn't watch.

The father of one of the apocalyptic kids, Jeff, was a NYC cop, so I assumed that encounters with crowd control and deadly force would be regular dining room table talk at their place. The other boys just seemed delighted by the wildness and autonomy they exercised as they headed daily toward the woods and began chopping trees and smashing things.

The ringleader was a tall, skinny kid with a concave chest named Joe Swain. He had been sent to a military academy only to return with stories of badassery and a crew cut. He was impressively adept at twirling a rifle. He demonstrated on a thick length of wood and everyone needed to try. They all chopped their own yard-long sticks from arm- thick limbs and practiced until they were flipping and catching more often than clocking themselves in the head. Someone coined the sticks, "Bufords," after the club-wielding sheriff in the film, *Walking Tall.*

I went to the woods on my own, fashioned my own Buford, and endured my share of jammed thumbs and bumps on the head as I twirled in private. It was fun and about as close to military anything that I ever cared to get. Joe's followers headed to the barber for crew cuts and to the Army/Navy store for fatigues and machetes. Joe always seemed to hate me. I can't remember a single time when he addressed me directly. The most I got was a squinty glare in my general direction accompanied by a slight smile. He displayed the kind of quiet that you'd expect from a serial killer. I was scared of him.

Wandering into the woods behind these guys one day, they took to picking on me, the youngest, making fun of my longer hair and calling me faggot. A couple of them began playfully pushing me. The pushing became shoving and Joe yelled something about me being the weakest link. Someone said, "tie him up," and in the next beat I was backed up to a tree, my hands tied behind me, thick twine being wrapped around me from my ankles to my throat. They laughed and, good sport that I was, I laughed along. Joe yelled to get leaves and they gathered them around my feet while another guy crumpled up balls of newspaper and stuffed them into my pant legs and between my feet.

Joey took out a lighter. He held it lit a few feet from my face and for the first time ever, he looked me in the eye. The crew held their collective breath as he squatted and ignited one of the balls of paper.

"Gentlemen ... pull out."

And they headed deeper into the woods, the fire catching around and beneath my feet. Cedrick Williams took a few steps after them, said, "guys, cut it out!" He lumbered back to my tree and me, stomped out the fires, opened a long pocketknife and cut me loose. Embers had spread so together we stomped and then peed on whatever glowing bits remained. We both took a chest full of the thick smoke and while my stinging eyes were wet I took the opportunity to cry my fear, my anger and my shame.

The Trouble With Kim

Cedrick and I, cast out of the reject militia, walked from the woods together. He wore a frown, certainly annoyed, but I suspect offended in other ways, being black and only a couple of generations away from similar antics that had been less random and which hadn't ended peacefully. We didn't speak until we split at the paths to our respective buildings.

"Bye," we said.

I recently reconnected with Cedd and thanked him for what he did. He remembers it differently. He said that he was one of the ones who planned and executed the plan, that he was sorry and that he hoped I wasn't plotting to kill him.

He liked my version better.

It was confusing and hurtful to hear him say that the act was premeditated. That I was a boy among boys, singled out to be the object of hatred and sadism.

I care less now about what people think about me. I know that my concerns about fitting in somewhere or other are the product of my own lack of self-esteem. Age, therapy and love have made this immeasurably clearer, but I can't help thinking that I had a virtual "kick me" sign pinned to my back.

I asked a friend why she thought I'd been so weak. She said that I wasn't. I was vulnerable.

Cory, 1979 - AGE FOURTEEN

BRIAN WAS A character. He lived in a three story building adjacent to a couple of school buddies of mine, and asked me to go record shopping downtown. We loved the same music and it was refreshing to spend time with someone new, someone nice. He was three years older than us, but we related well and we laughed a lot. He was one of the military kids and had stacks of gun magazines and owned several knives in the apartment he shared with his single mother. I found the weapons frightening but acted interested as I thought that this was what real boys did. We hung out that whole summer when I was fourteen and he was seventeen.

He'd befriended a girl who was in between our ages and early one heat wave morning we went to Manhattan to meet her. Her name was Cory and the apartment was in a dilapidated building on Sullivan Street. We spent a little awkward while in her room and as we headed for the door she bent over the couch where I hadn't even noticed a body and said, "Mom, I'm goin' out." Her mom was skinny and pretty with messed up skin. She couldn't have been more than 30. "Don't stay out late," she slurred, though it was still before noon. She nodded out before her head, lowering slowly, even hit the TV guide.

We walked around, sharing a beer with a straw from a brown bag. We got Italian ices and the two of them walked hand in hand. I trailed a few steps behind and was dispirited by jealousy. She was beautiful, with greasy short hair and brown crying eyes. I liked her a lot.

We got exhausted and hot and returned to Cory's place where we filled coffee mugs with chilly tap water and brought them up to the roof. Unlike the building where I grew up which had seven stories and a roof from which you could see Manhattan and Queens and Brooklyn in between, this roof sat just above the canopy of lush downtown trees, across from and above windows and fire escapes, Hell's Angels and squirrels. I felt like I could live right there forever. All the electricity, art and dirt I craved without having to look anyone in the eye.

The edge had no fence or gate, just a slight incline where I knelt and then lay down on my stomach, fingers and chin dangling, hot roof on my belly, burning sun on my back.

Brian and Cory were on another part of the roof and from the sound of it, probably fooling around. I grew suddenly pissed off at Brian. Their giggles stung and I got very sad and wanted to go home, but not to my home. The home I knew was hopeless, joyless and harsh.

With nowhere to go I quickly imagined a scene where I got up and kissed Cory (though I still wasn't sure how to kiss) followed by a slow motion run for the edge and a swan dive into oblivion, leaving them both stunned and regretful. Or I could do a handstand right there at the edge; that would impress Cory. Then once I had her attention I'd arch back, allow my weight to carry me street-ward, passing through the maple leaves and landing on the wrought-iron fence below, folded in half backwards, impaled and dead like that angel-dust girl whose picture I'd seen in the Village Voice. I could just be done with it.

Raindrops hit my back and then thunder ... *BOOM!* I heard the staircase door open and shut as Brian and Cory got out of the surprise downpour. I lifted my elbows and prepared to push my body up to standing and get to shelter but when I pushed off, the resistance was surprisingly great. I felt very heavy. Wind was whipping and rain pouring and I was completely stuck.

After some fruitless struggle, I realized that just an hour earlier; I had in fact lain down on a hot tar roof. And now I was trapped in inches of soft tar, glued to the hot roof.

In seconds I was drenched. And stuck. I squirmed and contorted and was able to peel myself up, leaving bits of fabric and drool where I had lived and died for the past hour.

I got inside the rooftop door and those two laughed when they saw me, wet, tarred and torn up. They laughed their asses off and I was compelled to run out the door toward my original plan. I stood frozen and ashamed, and just before I was about to cry, Cory took my hand and gave a soft tug.

She led me down the steps, her laugh trailing off but her lovely smile persisting, to her apartment, to her bathroom where she locked the door. She got me a couple of towels and helped me dry off, get undressed, then into a Motörhead t-shirt and a pair of her junkie-moms dry cut off jean shorts. She ripped fistfuls of long strawberry-blonde hair out of her brush and smiled as she ran it through my still-wet mop.

The Trouble With Kim

Then she kissed me.

I have no recollection of her beyond that moment.

But that's not what's important.

We tend think of salvation as something that would arrive in the form of a spirit-animal or an arc or a winning lottery ticket. But I've been saved more times than I've earned. A few times by an injured bird who needed my help more than I needed to cower in my own private purgatory. A few thousand times by a radio song that reminded me that I'm not the only one who feels.

And I believe that on this day I was granted a stay of execution by a poor little punk girl who gave me the time of day.

And who, I think it may be fair to say, liked me.

BERKOWITZ, 1977 - AGE TWELVE

MY PARENTS WERE racist. It was a two faced malady I'd started off by accepting, as in one minute I'd be in the care of my black sitter, Edna or enjoying a snack my mom prepared for my best friend, Eddie and me, then in the next my dad would utter, "black bastard" as we drove past a neighbor he disliked.

Mom would sit drinking iced tea with my best friend's black mother and then cite race if the nightly news reported a crime alleged to have been committed by a black person.

I was uneasy about it. People of all shades, accents and beliefs surrounded us and while I know I had my ignorance and fear-based biases, I didn't agree and I assumed that I would do it differently.

In the mid 70s, I was scared like everyone else in Queens. I was young for the profile teen or young adult that was being shot by the so called .44 Caliber Killer, but there was enough mass hysteria to have me believe I could easily get in the way and end up dead. It was all happening within miles of our home. My parents and neighbors were freaking out and it was the first time I'd felt this sort of terror. Police sketches depicted a young man whose face scarily resembled my brother's. This disturbed him but confounded my mother for a different reason. The suspect was white or Hispanic and she'd grown accustomed to blaming black men for the worst of violent crime in our society. She even said that he looked Puerto Rican.

When they caught Son of Sam we were pinned to the news. We saw police escorting a white guy (he did look like my brother) down to booking. They said his name was David Berkowitz. I was actually thrilled that he was a Jew. My mother shook her head and muttered, "Look at this crazy guy," and "What a nut."

"Why didn't you call him a "white bastard?" I asked.

She glared at me.

When investigators revealed that Berkowitz had been adopted as a child and was actually born to an Italian mother, my mother breathed a sigh of relief.

Cigarette, 1980 - Age Fifteen

Mom quit smoking the same year that congress required all cigarette packages distributed in the United States to carry a health warning. Everyone already knew it was harmful but the government shaking its finger at my mom was all it took for her to quit the stuff. From then on, she sought comfort from other, less immediately cancerous sources, especially ice cream bars, French Fries, very sweet Long Island Iced Teas, and Valium. I was told that until the time she quit smoking, she'd smoked around a pack a day.

A dozen years later, at a wedding of a kid of an old friend of hers in the Catskills, I came back from a bathroom trip and she had a cigarette in one hand and a drink in the other. She noticed me staring at her in utter disapproval and after a few tense moments said, "Gimme a break" and took a drag.

Dad, on the other hand, was not going to stop. Everything about him said that he smoked. The car was always filled with smoke. He smoked at breakfast. He smoked while watching the news and he smoked while sitting on the toilet in the middle of the night; there were always bloated cigarette filters in our toilet surrounded by a cloud of yellow-brown water, which I'd blast apart with sharpshooter precision when peeing.

Sam, the cat, loved Dad and would curl up against him during the six o'clock news. A pre-cuddle ritual included

The Trouble With Kim

Sam approaching, Dad reaching out and Sam recoiling after sniffing Dad's yellow-stained fingers, then easing his was to Dad's lap where accept gentle strokes in compromise.

Birthday and holiday gifts often included an ashtray I'd gotten at the school fair, some with cute animals or a snarky messages.

Many times I asked him to stop and he responded by saying that he would. He meant it, I know.

I began collecting the packs I could find and throwing them out the window of our fourth floor apartment. He yelled at me and went to retrieve them. I began to crumple them in my hands before tossing them, soaking them in water, flushing and hiding them. It felt playful to me and I hoped that he'd just get my reasoning and my love and be done with the stuff. I thought that the more elaborate my show of love, the more healing would result.

Once, I inserted tiny explosive "loads" into my dad's cigarettes and sat quietly as the ash grew. The loud crack startled my heart-patient dad and sent bits of burning ash into his face, one landing squarely in his eye. He jumped to his feet and screamed, Mom rushing to see what had happened and asking me what the hell I was thinking. When I saw that he was going to live, I retreated, crying, to my room. I heard him complaining about me, and Mom telling him to stay still while she nursed him back to health. There was quiet for a minute or so and I heard the next small explosion. Dad was quiet and I could hear Mom's slippers coming down the foyer. The door swung open and we stared at each other until she cracked a smile.

My dad was stuck. He wanted to live, to feel good, and to be with our family. But these were overruled by his need for nicotine and the rest of it. Had I abstained from my loving gestures we all could have just gone on living with smoke, feeling whatever, our bodies suffering the same first and second hand consequences as we actually did. I could have spared him the added guilt and me the succession of punishments that I endured with regularity, every one discouraging (but not eradicating) my heroism, all in the name of love and preservation.

As repulsive as his habit was, as much as I vowed never to be like dad, to never do the vile things that he did, I did, of course, become a smoker. Cigarettes occasionally, but marijuana constantly, for years.

When Dad was receiving treatment for prostate cancer at Sloan Kettering in Manhattan, I commuted in after school, went straight into the bathroom in the lobby, and lit a joint. (This was before smoke detectors were uniformly installed in public bathrooms that prohibited smoking).

I'd light up when going for a middle of the night pee. I smoked at work, smoked at the wheel, and smoked right up until meeting any of my friends or my family. I owned that I could only be "myself" when I was high and stayed that way all the time.

When, on occasion, I would decide to quit, I'd try to force myself in some of the same ways that had failed to work for Dad. I threw my weed out the car window while driving (only to return later in attempts to retrieve it). I wet it, tossed it and flushed it. I'd make promise to my myself and count the hours until bed, saying I only have that many more hours, that I can make it that long, only to head out and break that promise. Again.

Dad hated himself for smoking. I know that he felt weaker every time he failed, each time he told me he would quit, and then didn't. I understand this sort of low, this inadvertent, suicidal trap. I'm so sad that he had to live this way.

Dad on the other hand smoked right up until a team of doctors and nurses screamed at him for lightning up while on oxygen at Lenox Hill Hospital where he had just had a heart attack during an exploratory heart procedure.

With nurses back at their stations and doctors continuing rounds, Dad had climbed out of the bed, untied the plastic bag containing his personal belongings, found his soft pack of Kents, and lit up. His cardiac arrest resumed just as he was caught. In the remaining twenty years of his life, as far as I know, he never smoked again.

A Bit About Dad

I USED TO get sick quite often. Although sore throats and strep were my forte, I had headaches all the time and got pretty good at vomiting. One of my parents would detect my nausea and head downstairs to the soda man who regularly drove a truck through the project with warm soda and seltzer bottles for sale or exchange. They'd return with the understanding that the sugary elixir would heal me. We rarely had soda in the fridge so this was a confusing thing for little me: get sick, get rewarded. Versions of this contradictory rhetoric would play a part in my life for many years to come.

I vividly remember shouting for my father from bed as I felt a sickness coming on. He stumbled out of his own sleepy place to my bedside just in time to cup his hands and catch my first round of puke. He then carried it off to the bathroom a few steps away, deposited it in the toilet, did a quick wash up and returned to my side with the bucket and a damp towel. It was pretty badass. I now assume it was as much to spare my mother the trouble of a soiled carpet as it was a reflex, like catching a falling knife. My dad loved me and he was cool.

I never doubted the former, but quickly forgot the latter.

When kids at school boasted about how good their dads were at softball or basketball, how strong or tall or funny they were or about their cool jobs, I kept quiet. I could utilize my brother, being ten years my senior, as a source of bragging rights, citing his speed, musicianship, record collection, martial artistry, and intelligence. I was quite proud. I couldn't get enough of him and he certainly loved me but after a minute of me wanting him to play with every ounce of my seven year old energy, he was teen-overwhelmed and would tell me to leave him alone. I'd be hurt and call my parents and shit would fly. There was no way for us to fill each other's needs but I felt regularly confused and banished to a life as both baby brother and only child. He was a complicated hero.

My father was neither fit nor ambitious. He was hotheaded, uncultured and not well read. His entire existence seemed to be a struggle to keep jobs, ward off bill collectors and defend his inadequacies. His hospitalizations were long and mysterious and their frequency somehow justified his underachieving in my mind, and I assume in his.

Coming home in the evening, he'd sit at the dinette table and begin to dial.

"Operator, I dialed a wrong number three times. Yes, of course I'd like credit."

"Good afternoon, my name is Branitz and I have a bill here for blood work that insurance is supposed to pay. Well I suggest you resubmit it. Submit it again.

Lady, who's side are you on? *I'M* the customer!"

"Hello, my name is Branitz ... B-R-A-N-I-T-Z, Branitz.

I have a cut off notice here. *Didn't you* receive my check? Several days ago. Maybe a week. I just need to be sure I'm not gonna get cut off. Well I paid ... aren't you listening to me? What's you name, please? Are you upset with me? Did I do something to make you angry with me? Well it sounds like it."

These nickel and dime acts of survival sought to raise my father's bruised ego just off the mat where his financial ass had been counted out, but also to let my mother, brother and me know that he was willing to fight. He really believed that he was a victim and that the world had it out for him.

Once, when I was eight, he came down to the park with me so we could throw a pink Spalding ball. I played no sports and was afraid to be asked to play with the kids, so I welcomed this unthreatening chance and felt happy at the prospect of having fun with my dad. I bounced the ball by myself until he walked twenty or thirty feet away and I threw it to him. He chased my wild throw down and turned to return it with what looked more like a spastic shot-put than a throw. The ball bounced only part of the way back to me before flattening to a roll. I picked it up, walked to him and said I wanted to go. He asked, "already?" and I said yes, that we should do something upstairs. I put my arm around his waist and he put his on my shoulder and we headed home, each ashamed of his inability to throw a ball but quietly bound by forgiveness.

My father often spoke of playing pool on the East Side and claimed to have been a champion of some manner back when he was a young man. If in the presence of a pool table at a restaurant or when watching a pool tournament on TV, he would say how much he would love to have his own pool table. Among the things I would hope to eventually buy for him, a pool table was a close second to a Medium Blue Metallic Delta 88, a car and color he admired whenever we passed one but which would remain out of his league.

During one of his convalescences, he spent time volunteering for a program at a state park, cataloging indigenous plants, cleaning trails, and I don't really know what the hell he was doing there because he talked a lot of shit that none of us was ever really sure was true or not. As winter approached he went out for walks and would sometimes be gone for a couple of hours.

At dinner one evening my father told my mother and me that he'd been shooting pool at the Queens College Student Union building nearby. Solo mostly, but also with some college age "Oriental kids" whose skills he found impressive. Some faculty member had watched him play, struck up a conversation and asked Dad if he would be interested in teaching a workshop on the game. My father, who had always, to the best of my recollection been simple and resigned to his station somewhere short of mediocracy, and who's jobs had never lasted longer than a couple of years (exterminator, parking lot attendant, checker-cab driver, postal mail sorter...) was owning this assignment and didn't blink an eye at the notion. Mom and I were stunned beneath our smirks and soon began eight weeks of Thursdays where groups of college students who had seen the fliers posted at the Student Union gathered to learn the basics of pool from an bona-fide champion (Dad claimed to have been champion of his pool hall on the Lower East Side during the Coca-Cola sponsored tournaments featuring an exceptional player named The Masked Marvel (several ace players wore that mask over time, I've come to find) who toured pool halls across the nation during the thirties and forties, expanding the Coca Cola brand, defeating hustlers and wearing a mask. When the poster went up, the owners of the pool hall signed Dad up. As the story goes, the masked guy got to break and racked up an impressive score before missing the eight ball. On dad's turn he ran the table and became the hero of the neighborhood.

I went to watch him school his enthusiastic protégés on two occasions. Dad was generously present, calmly explaining set ups and shots, demonstrating with effortless precision and reviewing the basics of breaking, using the bridge, bank shots, and English. For every young person who was signed up for his course there were five more curiously freeloading in the wings or watching from their own tables. My father, who was good at nothing (and, if you believed our downstairs neighbor, Mr. Sermon, was good "for" nothing), was amazing.

Dad was asked to do another eight weeks but didn't feel up for it. He'd done something which was simultaneously so very out of character and which fit like a glove.

The gravity of his aching body and the bullies of his mind necessitated more hospitalizations, more public assistance, and a secure place on the bottom rung of the ladder of inadequacy. Without even yet knowing how to negotiate my own way, I longed for *him* to find, to acknowledge and to enjoy his purpose. To help others and to have fun in the process. To be light, confident, connected, to be really good at something. He'd felt it as a young man, and then again for a minute.

I like to think that life can be an agreeable transaction, that the ledger makes concessions for lightness as well as the other, for take as well as for give. Dad was many shades of bankrupt and we all suffered his dynamic misfortune. But for a few minutes at times, he was also brave. Good at something. Heroic. Cool.

I'm sure that it might have helped him not to actually *be* more or *do* better, but to be recognized for whatever greatness he already has. From that standpoint, it was my eyes as much as his own that failed him.

Vigils

ON THE DAY when coverage of the Viet Nam War's official end dominated the news, I was on our couch with my mother, whose eyes were glued to the set.

"Is it over?" I asked.

"Sort of."

"Who won?"

"We lost."

My parents argued constantly and were allied in an unintentional undoing of my brother through intolerance, disapproval and withholding. My brother's efforts would never please our dad, haunted as he was by his own dereliction. There were broken things and holes in doors and I once failed to break them apart in time to save my dad a trip to the ER with a couple of broken ribs at my brother's hands (his right foot, to be exact). A particularly nasty fight between my brother and me ended with him screaming in pain and throwing furniture around the living room after I landed a right, flush in his eye socket. He dragged himself to the room past our crying mother.

I went to sleep on the couch and wouldn't return to the room we had shared for three years. I didn't greet him or listen to music with him or give him the satisfaction of being at the table for a family meal if he was there. I hated him. I shunned his efforts to reconcile, experimenting with power over my big brother, building my case. This troubled

74

our parents, but as each of us were certain that we were right, there was no wiggle room.

Kim shook me awake late on December 8. I was on my couch and I ignored him, making believe I was not wake-able.

"Wake up ... Seth ... wake up ... someone shot John Lennon."

I sat up. "Is he ok?"

"He might die."

We sat together in the dark, and for the first time in a good chunk of both of our lives, talked. We argued over Beatles songs, talked about our family, and a truce was implied.

Alone, I took the bus to the train to Manhattan and walked a long way to The Dakota (the Lennon residence). Right across the street in Central Park there was a gathering at a place now called Strawberry Fields. There were thousands there, each in love with music and with John and with the illusion of peace, talking to strangers and generous in their grief. We stood through the ten minutes of silence poor Yoko had called for, during which all that could be heard were sniffles and helicopters. A man screamed, "get those choppers outa here!" just as the first chords of Imagine blared through the speakers.

When I was ten I asked my dad what would happen if Kim got drafted. He said that he wouldn't let him go. Having heard about consequences for dodging the draft, I asked just what he would do. He said he'd move to Canada or he would hide him and that he was willing to face jail, but that he wouldn't let either of his sons go to war. I felt for him even then, unspoken grief and shock therapy behind him, years of struggle ahead, knowing that if the call came, he could do nothing.

I feel just like my dad, wanting with all my resolve to protect my boys from the draft but knowing that my heart will not get the job done and that I'm too stuck to move to Canada.

I know that good is there, here, all around us. I plug into it by doing good things, considering the welfare of others, making stuff. I doubt that any of this makes up for skills which I lack, but it's how I approach my work, my parenting, my healing, my big questions. I focus on my art and my music and my sons and on cleaning up my messes and on making smaller ones going forward. The world doesn't care that I care. I can only make peace where I stand and ask the world to get along and I can envision lives lived fully by each and every soldier and senator. And maybe I can make peace with the absence of peace.

With matter over mind.

With choppers over vigils.

FALCON, 1980 - AGE FOURTEEN

DAD'S CARS WERE always the oldest on the block. They were rusty and dented. He'd cover cracked lights and reflectors with duct tape which would eventually unstick and hang when parked, flailing once up to speed. There were these shady guys that would drive around the supermarket parking lots and offer to fix dents for a reasonable fee. They'd puncture and pull some of them out, and others they'd just patch up with some sort of putty. The fix resulted in an improvement but still looked ugly, especially if, as in my dad's case, they remained unpainted.

When I was in high school, Dad found a mechanic he liked and trusted on Jamaica Avenue in Queens Village near where my girlfriend lived. It was further from home than made sense to me, but they got the job done. The mechanic scared me. He was very loud and seemed to never blink. Dad's business with him had recently dealt with his green 1962 Ford Falcon.

I came home one day and Mom and Dad were silent and tense. I asked what was wrong and Mom said that Dad had a fight with his mechanic. Dad had brought the car back after a mechanical symptom had returned saying that whatever it was that he'd paid to do was obviously not done. The guy fixed it, citing an additional problem and charging my dad for the new repair. Dad got furious, called him a fucking crook and drove off in the car without paying.

When my mother and I tried to show him that he owed the guy for work he did, he told us we were turning on him, paced the room like he was being attacked, and walked out on us. We were both embarrassed by my father's behavior but figured he'd just have to find another mechanic. We hoped there would be someone trustworthy closer to home this time.

In the morning my mom woke me from a stoned sleep saying, "Seth ... sorry, Seth ... we have an emergency ... Dad can't find his car."

In the projects we had a handful of blocks and driveways to park on and some were restricted on certain days for certain hours and so it wasn't unusual to walk for a few minutes or more only to realize you were a block in the other direction.

But Dad had walked the entire maze and still couldn't find his car. I got up and ran up and back myself, only to verify that the car was not there.

Our suspicion was that the mechanic who my father had ripped off the day before had taken the car. My dad could barely speak but together we filed a police report, leaving out that he had taken the car without paying. I said, "They had a disagreement over services rendered."

My dad saw life as a big hand that just kept slapping him in the face and this time the hand was a fist. He was broke and had no idea where to turn. His trusted mechanic was now an adversary. The police saw no urgency. Dad had no allies who could help with this. He was really bad at doing things that involved change.

When I was a brand new driver I crashed my dad's car and when I told him and my mom, he was beyond pissed off, … he was wounded. I watched from our fourth floor living room window as he approached the car to assess the damage, and walked around to the driver's side where he viewed the caved in door. He screamed something incoherent and started kicking the car in broad daylight.

It was standard practice to try and avoid making my dad crazy, but again I'd failed.

My brother and I were regularly credited with one of my Dad's breakdowns or another. It was part of my mom not being able to cope with the plain reality that he was fucking crazy.

I still have a tough time when someone close to me is unsteady or unstable. I have to remind myself that I am not the reason. I'm not always calming, supportive and neutral, but everyone's crazies are their own.

It's no surprise that I also inherited this particular grade of unease and nausea specifically reserved for car issues. I hear a knock from the wheel well or a dashboard light goes on and there's a simultaneous meltdown and I'm desperate and panicked and fucked.

A week or so after the car disappeared our doorbell rang. The police stayed in the hallway and told dad that they'd found the car that afternoon. It had been fished out of Kissena Park Lake, a polluted nearby body of water my family took strolls around on nice days. Dad just stared at the officers. Mom, who had ridden a bicycle only once as a girl but had never learned to drive, did the talking, thanked them and led my dad to their room where he lay down and went to sleep.

I wanted to kill the guy who'd done this to my poor, crazy father.

But at the same time, I couldn't blame him.

First Time, 1979 - age fourteen

ON THE NIGHT of my fourteenth birthday I headed to the city to lose my virginity. I wanted nothing more than to feel as if I was wanted and that life was worthwhile. I saw it as a way to circumvent the desolation waiting for me in the apartment I shared with my disillusioned, depressive and drug addicted parents and brother. All were self-abusers. All were fending for themselves. I was screaming for love and for balance, for validation and autonomy. I was drafting suicide notes and considering the respect I'd finally receive from classmates and neighbors, postmortem.

I was fighting for my life, and I needed to get laid.

The way it was supposed to happen, Brian and I would take the bus to Forest Hills, grab the E-train to the West 4th Street station in Greenwich Village, and walk across Sixth Avenue and into the West Village neighborhood where he had arranged the whole thing. He'd done it himself just a week before, after meeting a guy in his thirties, being offered the chance to have sex, and going to a studio apartment where the guy furnished him with a girl. Brian said that he'd had sex with her and didn't have to pay. The guy was cool and the place was clean.

The only thing, he said, was that the guy took some pictures. That small hitch didn't deter my lustful resolve, and when Brian asked if I wanted to go with him and do the same, I accepted his offer. He was three years older than

I, so I was sure that he had it all worked out. I felt better knowing Brian would be there. He would keep me safe. I saw no other way to accomplish this feat on my own—not for years at least. I didn't like the idea of having my picture taken, but was seduced by the fabulous opportunity being set out before me. I just kept my eye on the prize.

The blocks were short and narrow, every few streetlights were out, and almost all the pedestrians were men. It's the first time I can remember being aware of my heart beating so hard I could feel it in my entire torso. I was worried about what I would say to the girl—my first—and hoped she would be pretty. When we arrived at the brick building, Brian said I should wait outside while he got plans straight with Martin. I paced, cold in my t-shirt and black leather jacket and confused by the looks I got from passersby. Guys walked by, huddled together and more than one stared at me too long. One made a purring sound, which brought giggles from his friend.

Brian finally returned with manic energy, hopping up and down in the cold. We walked up two flights of stairs and through a door with five locks. Martin wore thick glasses, had longish, wavy dark hair, and was nerdy. He looked nervous, as if he was anxious to impress me and was trying too hard. I felt somehow important. He asked us to sit on his bed, got us beers and talked too much. After a while, he and Brian began to discuss what he did there. He said that he just liked to watch people have sex and take pictures of them. He picked up one of a few Polaroid cameras that had been sitting on a dresser.

"Smile!" He pressed the button. Click-whirrr, went the camera as it spit out its raw square of memory. He was weird, I thought, but harmless.

As if I was being invited to a cool party or a private screening, he asked if I was going to partake.

I said yes.

I had no idea that there was another answer I could have given. It didn't occur to me to engage my integrity or consider potential danger, or even my own discomfort, and excuse myself. I was already at a disadvantage being so young, if I were also rude or uncool I would have embarrassed Brian and myself, *and* missed out on this life-changing offer. I was sure that an enthusiastic *yes!* was the only real answer, that whatever I was feeling was wrong, and that full speed ahead was right.

Martin put his hands, prayer-like, against his heart. "Oh, goodie!."

I was sure that they knew what they were doing and that I was going to be taken care of.

First, Brian left Martin and I alone to shoot some pictures—click-whirrr. I was initially freaked out by the idea but my inebriation guided me. He instructed me in a variety of poses and then, as if it was already agreed upon, he climbed onto the bed. I'm sure there was no way to avoid reading my body language as I tensed up entirely. He assured me. "Don't worry, I'm not gonna kiss ya."

He did not kiss me.

We finished and got dressed. Brian came back and

there soon appeared at the door a teenaged girl Martin had invited over in order to give me what I came for, I assumed. I would come to learn she was compensated for her services. She was small, tough and cute and told me— in the course of progressing through logical next steps, "No kissing." It wasn't until years later that I heard an actress playing a prostitute in a movie saying those same words and I recalled her voice and the feeling of casual rejection with absolute clarity.

The next hours are a rushed jumble of freezing cold, nausea, bodies nearby and against mine, and panic. I felt trapped. Three or four of us were always on the bed and I ached to be outside, walking the streets, anywhere but here. I kept my eyes mostly closed and when I opened them I was unable to make sense of the many unfamiliar hands and undulating body parts there in the spinning studio. There was Martins Polaroid—click-whirrr—shooting me from every angle and dodging, naked between them.

Like three rubber Lego pieces, Brian and she cycled me through various configurations, a minute here, an eternity there. Martin kept joining in then hopping off the bed, appearing in blurs or behind the click-whirrr of one of his cameras, changing packs of film countless times. I was frozen.

I have since seen, imagined, and taken part in three and four-way sexual exchanges that I found thrilling, beautiful or both. This was not one of those.

I was paralyzed by surprise, shame, revulsion, and an innate need to make sure that no one present knew this. It seems like they all acted either on an assumption that I was into it or that what I thought didn't matter, although there was nothing to make them think I liked it, or that I was good at it. Clearly I was not, evidenced by several playful comments from the girl and comparisons I could not avoid making between Brian's body and my own. Nothing about me was good enough for this encounter, yet there were these three confident and experienced fuckers minding and mining me with animalistic enthusiasm.

Knowing that I was supposed to be on-board and excited but unable to gain any traction whatsoever, I smashed my eyes so tightly and for so long that they hurt for days. At one point, I pinned my lips together, teeth nearly cutting through, to discourage anything from entering my mouth.

I could have gotten up, gotten dressed and left. I could have verbalized, "Stop" or even asked for something different that interested me. I now expect that they might have complied—they weren't vicious. They could have seen that I was confused, lost and grossed out. A cold prospect. A poor candidate. A kid who wasn't into it.

It went on forever.

Click-whirr...

After they were done and we were all dressed, Martin said he wanted to show me something and opened the kitchen cabinets to reveal hundreds of polaroid prints, fun-tacked to the inside panels. Every one featured a young man within a few years of my age, nude, posing alone or in some act of cuddling, kissing or touching another. Few of them were smiling. He said that he'd gotten some great ones of me and that I would now join the club. He seemed excited to have had me.

The girl left and a friend of Martins arrived, a tall, beautiful woman with full, shiny shoulder-length dark hair, a three-quarter-length raincoat, fishnet stockings and heels. She looked like a sexy private eye or something out of a porn mag. Martin introduced her as Sandy and she held her large, limp hand out as if expecting to have it kissed rather than shaken. Her arrival was a very welcome distraction and I liked her. She was elegant, street smart, and funny. Martin asked her to show us her latest development and she took off her cost to reveal a sheer blouse through which we could see her large, firm tits. I'd spent my entire adolescence sneaking glances at my favorite body parts, but here was Sandy, putting them on display for me to inspect and I found it hard to do. Martin clapped and told her they were wonderful. Sandy, hands on hips, pulled her shoulders back accentuating their protrusion. They were amazing, like nothing I'd ever seen, and as I was learning, they were brand new. They talked for a bit and Martin mentioned that the young girl who'd just left seemed like a "street kid" and said that she seemed dirty. Sandy asked how I felt and I said I was fine. She said that if I experience any pain when trying to pee, I should go to the doctor. I couldn't get my mind around certain clues about Sandy, and began to suspect that she was a man. Martin and she occupied different corners of some dark sexual underground where I now found myself, buzzed, numb, and used. Brian later confirmed Sandy's gender of origin. I couldn't imagine her being part of acts as manipulative and depraved as what I'd just experienced, but then again, I wouldn't have guessed Martin had it in him. When Sandy turned to leave I was sad. Now I was alone with Brian and Martin. Sandy's attention had been welcome. It was the first and only time during the entire ordeal that someone seemed to care about my needs, to be interested in who I was.

Brian made a manic spectacle of himself on the train ride home, laughing and acting more drunk than he was. I only remember shivering and wishing he would sit down and shut up. We hung out a few days later and I watched us both dodge the subject nervously. We finally landed on the acknowledgment that something had indeed transpired and could do nothing but explore a bit more, getting interrupted once by a local kid who had come knocking on the door with a stack of new records under his arm. Brian was paranoid and afraid that he would blow our cover.

Our friendship seemed to be over, and I felt very lonely and abandoned. I was left with a ton of shame and confusion about how such a thing could have happened and about who I was.

We didn't see each other for a while and then Brian called and asked me to meet him in the stairwell of my building. He was panicking as he said that something was wrong with him—that he couldn't get off without thinking about guys. Then he begged me to have sex with him right there, which I didn't want to do. He started to disrobe but before negotiations progressed, we heard a door open on one of the floors beneath and he pulled himself together and sprinted up the stairs to the roof, slamming the door behind him. I heard the rooftop gravel crushing under his military boots as he scampered to the reentry door of the adjoining building. I was completely dumbfounded and totally alone. I never saw or heard from Brian again.

A thousand times I've replayed alternative outcomes of a courageous and self-assured me, ones in which I noticed that this was not what I'd agreed to and was unafraid to speak up. But I wouldn't just leave, I'd strike out, leaving the men bloody and the girl backed up and impressed, respectful, and now somehow interested in having that taboo kiss. I plotted to return to Martins' apartment, to beat and bind him, leave him there to suffer and regret, to fear and to die. I imagined myself walking calmly down the street, away from the building as fire raged from the windows, the sound of floors collapsing down over his duct-taped, bruised and burning body.

I spent a lot of time hating.

I confided in no one and lived with this secret and with a crushing fear that I was a freak. I had done something awful. Something shameful. Something I would not be able to live down. A face tattoo. A murder.

I buried my story and hid my terror, as AIDS dominated the headlines and men in our community began showing signs of infection, and then later in early recovery when they began dropping all around me. I feared testing positive as much for becoming gravely ill as for the threat it would certainly impose on any potential legacy. I felt diseased and horrible.

The Trouble With Kim

I never sought actual revenge, and am sure that Martin is dead.

I just recently began thinking about this incident objectively. Even now, my focus isn't so much on what happened TO ME. At the time, the possibility of me being gay was terrifying. It was something I misunderstood, and between societal ignorance and schoolyard name-calling, it was something I couldn't bear. I had no problem with YOU being gay, but not me. No way. My gay thing was sneaky and shameful and wrong, steeped in life ruining, reputation damaging secrets. Click-whirrr. I never even considered that I was a good person who'd experienced an unfortunate thing or that maybe I simply fancied both attractive females and males. Such innocuous deviations were not easily accepted all those years ago.

My focus had long been on the weight that I thought my participation in this incident had had on my worth and on my karma. It isn't until decades later, though, that I review these events with veils lifted, and a couple of new considerations come to mind:

Was I betrayed?

Brian knew exactly what was supposed to happen and roped me in at Martins request, so yes.

Was he paid? Was he asked to find the weakest among his friends? How did he know I wouldn't run out on them or make a scene?

Was I raped? My stiff body and non-participation said, "No" even if my voice didn't. I was a kid.

Seth Branitz

✳ ✳ ✳ ✳ ✳

The last time I tried to donate blood was in the 90's. I was told that because I answered "yes" to a certain question on the blood-bank intake form, I would not be allowed to donate. I was healthy and strong, balanced and disease-free, but was turned away as a matter of public safety. I could not contribute said wellness to some person in need, and likely never would because I was "a man who engaged in sex with another man..." during the time period when the virus was being most rampantly spread. All these years later, healthy, HIV negative and not promiscuous, I couldn't contribute.

When my son asked if I would come and donate at his middle-school blood drive where he was volunteering, I told him that I couldn't. He asked why I said I'd tell him another time. We've had discussions about sex and sexuality but never this.

The evening he returned from putting in his blood drive hours, he came home, headed right to me and asked for the answer I'd promised. I hesitated only for an instant and then felt no need to qualify my response or to attach any ugly to the truth. I told him about question #9 on that long ago form and said that I couldn't answer No to the question about being a man who'd had sex with another man during the years in question. Unaffected, he asked, "Who was it?." I told him it was someone I'd never mentioned to him. He was satisfied, took off his sweatshirt and proceeded to tell me about his experience, signing adults up and guiding them to their respective phlebotomists. He said there were juice boxes and granola bars, and that he'd enjoyed it.

JUNE, 1981 - AGE SIXTEEN

I GOT MY first extemporaneous blowjob from a girl named June in the nosebleeds at a Billy Joel concert right before I started high school.

My older friends had called her the hottest girl at Jamaica High and when I met her I was surprised to see that she wasn't the particular type of vixen I'd envisioned. Small, with straight brown hair and very pretty, June was friendly and approachable, but had developed a reputation that filled a need for just that sort of legend.

I had planned to go with my friend, Leor and a girl he knew from school. When something came up, he gave his ticket to a second girl whose dad agreed drive us home after the show. The first friend was Eileen, with whom I had a couple of classes and a passive rapport. June was her school friend, although this would be their first time mixing socially.

We took the F train to Penn Station and, awkward in our own way as each of us was, the chatter dealt with rock bands we loved and teachers we hated. June suggested that we buy some booze and I followed her lead to the liquor store, where she captivated the Indian clerk with her smile, purchased a pint of blackberry brandy and walked out. Eileen and I were dumbfounded and we began swigging as the crowd thickened outside The Garden.

We got close to the gate and June grabbed the waistline

of my jeans and slid the flat bottle down into my crotch to hide it.

I got drunk and June got drunker, getting testy with some other teenage girls in the row in front of us. A few songs into the show, she turned to kiss me and lay a couple of hickeys on the side of my neck, one on my Adam's apple. This alone would have made my year, but her inhibitions vanished and she opened up my pants and went down on me. This left me with a difficult choice. I could allow the hottest girl in Jamaica High School to continue throwing herself at me, or I could ask her to stop, remind her that there were twenty thousand people in the room with us, and possibly give her the idea that we weren't on the same page.

While I weighed the wisdom of one choice over the other, I closed my eyes and slipped into an out-of-body experience. From several feet above, I could see the back of her head in my lap, Eileen glancing disapprovingly toward us, and an expanding concentric circle of music fans getting wind of the pornographic side show in section 426.

June sat up for a while, leaning into me as my arm wrapped around her shoulder. I became spacey and weightless from the brandy, mesmerized and moved by the music, and as I looked toward June, I did not see her. I scanned the area several times but where she had been I could now see straight through to Eileen. Then I realized that she was still right there next to me, only bent chest to thighs, throwing up. She could hardly stand and the previously hostile girls in front of us brought her to the ladies room and took care of her. Eileen and I followed, saying nothing until one of them stepped out into the now bustling hallway to report that June was just getting cleaned up, drinking some water and would be out in a minute. They were lovely.

June stumbled and slurred, hanging on me and Eileen all the way out of The Garden, onto the street and over to West 33rd street where her dad was to be picking us up. June's drunken laughing, hanging and eye rolling came to a complete halt as the brown Oldsmobile pulled up to the curb. She said, "Hi, Daddy," and we all got in. The spell was lifted and June was no longer inebriated or messy. She rattled off some highlights and her adoring father engaged us the whole way. I got dropped off near my building and went home to ponder what had transpired.

The next day I was questioned and drilled, my hickeys serving to leave no doubt as to the efficacy of my story. Word spread amongst the smaller circle of guys in the project, at least for a few days. My high school career began the following week and I looked high and low for June, who I didn't see for the first few weeks.

I expected that she'd resume the hot-girl persona and pay me no mind at all, dopey little sophomore that I was. When I eventually saw her in the hall between classes one day, she was laughing with a tall, handsome guy who looked to be a senior. I veered from the center of the hallway over to the right in order to avoid contact. I was embarrassed for our past and felt small and silly in the present.

I kept a safe distance a few more times until the day

Seth Branitz

I came face to face with her at the west entrance to the school building. I was going out while she was going in. We stood for a blank moment and then she opened her arms and hugged me. She shrunk down to size and lay the side of her face on my chest. I felt validated, not because this beautiful girl had had sex with me, but because for a moment it looked as if there was a chance she might be willing to be my friend.

June, The Sequel, 1981 - Age Sixteen

THE DOCTOR WAS an odd bird—a dead ringer for John Waters—with intense powers of observation, a pencil-thin mustache, and an indistinguishable accent. I was fifteen and he was a specialist we'd arrived at in an effort to diagnose and eliminate the painful swelling in my left armpit.

Life in our family seemed to be held together by doctor's visits and my nominal interest in this one was due to the fact that this time I was the patient. At first I thought that he was Spanish, but then he used a throaty, "cchhhh" sound, which led me to think he might have been Eastern European.

He pointed to the blemish on my forearm and said "And vhat is theees?" I told him that I'd had a huge boil. That one day, a few months earlier, while lifting a fifty-pound bag of flour at work, the growing pressure finally got relived with an audible "pop," sending puss and blood flying. I'd cleaned and medicated it, covered it and forgot about it. Aside from that, I had a lump beside by left temple, the source for which could be explained in several ways, but combined with the armpit thing, was suspect.

The doctor told Mom and me that he suspected one of two things, that either the boil had been infected; the infection had run up my arm and had come to fester in the lymph nodes under my arm, causing me pain and discomfort.

Or, he said evenly, it could be Hotchkins lymphoma.

The gravity of that possibility didn't make an impression on me. I suppose I was trusting that whatever it was, it could be fixed and that since I was young, nothing would happen to me. Mom, I would later learn, was petrified by the prospect of the often deadly, always difficult Hotchkins. My mother and two doctors coordinated a date for a lymphadenectomy and a lumpectomy and a few weeks later we two took a cab to Parkview Hospital in Forest Hills, walked to admissions, presented documents and sat down with a clipboard to fill out forms.

Just then, a teenage girl with a shopping bag, a pillow and a stuffed bear came into the admission area with her mother. She looked frightened and pale, and when we made eye contact, we both paused for a few seconds. June smiled and said hi first, then I followed suit, waving. Our mothers were as surprised as we were and smiled at one another.

June was there to have her tonsils removed. We hadn't spoken since the night we'd met, save a quick hug and hello in passing at school. How vulnerable a place to now find ourselves. We suddenly seemed like little kids.

I was to be there for a night and a day, during which I'd get prepped, have the strange surgeon deal with my lump and my lymph, and then recover for a couple more days. If all went well, I'd go home. If the nodes indicated a Hotchkins diagnosis, however, there would begin a plan B.

After I'd gotten settled in my room, Mom said good night and told me she'd be back before surgery the next morning.

I watched TV and hung out in a waiting room with

other adolescent patients. I played checkers with Kevin, a blonde boy a little younger than me. He was attached to a rolling IV and didn't speak. I talked about heavy metal with a chubby, pig-tailed girl wearing an Iron Maiden t-shirt over her hospital gown. And I got a kick out of a charming Italian kid a couple of years older than me. He'd had his spleen removed (this was the first I'd heard of a spleen) and I called him "Spleenless Matt," which he liked. He was tall and cocky and had great hair. He'd packed dirty magazines and showed them to Kevin and me in his room. Kevin's jaw dropped as he saw sights he may never before have considered. Certain images evoked involuntary grunts and I loved how unashamedly he shared and consumed them. He dropped open the centerfold and, as Kevin and I ogled, said "she can fott (fart) on my face any day of the week." I loved that. Later that day, as I left the room so a nurse could redress his wounds, he began to remove his gown and I saw dozens of large scars across his chest, stomach and back. Spleenless Matt had been here before.

We were encouraged back to our rooms. Mine had two beds but I was the only patient in it. I felt very alone without my mom to kiss goodnight and for the first time I began to worry about the state of my health. I'd completely ignored the chance that this was something bad, but now, in the solitude of my unfamiliar environs, I was beginning to panic. The TV was on but I wasn't able to redirect my thoughts.

I heard a knock and looked toward the door and June was standing there smiling in sweat pants and a tee shirt.

Her smile calmed me and she and her stuffed bear sat on the other bed and we talked for a while. We hushed ourselves repeatedly so as not to attract the attention of a nurse, and then she came onto my bed. We talked awhile more and then she got under the blankets with me. We connected powerfully that night, talking around our fear, ok with our awkwardness and eventually acknowledging that we once again had found ourselves in unusually close proximity.

I thought a lot about making a move and am sure it was on her mind as well. We settled on being bunkmates, frightened kids empowered by serendipity and the love of a virtual stranger.

After midnight a nurse sped into the room. She stared at us for a few seconds and let out an enormous sigh. She told us how alarmed she'd been while she thought she'd lost a patient. She said we were adorable and then gave us five more minutes to wrap it up. We exchanged addresses and June left.

There was no malignancy and I healed well. I assume that June's procedure was routine and that she was quickly recovered.

Although I knew June far less than any of the girls I kissed or loved, this might be the most intimate and vulnerable experience I had with any. After the hospital I thought about her all the time, then a bit less, and then moved on.

We exchanged letters for a few rounds, and then lost touch. That was that.

RAMBLER, 1981 - AGE SIXTEEN

I WAS SIXTEEN when my brother, Kim impulsively bought a rusty 1962 AMC Rambler.

He lived at home with our aging parents and wasn't working and was trying to finish up his long-winded philosophy degree. A habit of poor choices kept the fighting regular at home. Money and privacy infringement and disappointment and alcohol and drugs ... our mom was always writing him checks for unpaid parking ticket fines. Our dad always cursed him as he forked over the money my brother begged him for in order to maintain his insurance policies or pay private debt. Friends and drug buddies came calling at all hours and my parent's tolerance was being tested. This car raised all kinds of new hell.

She was light green, long, low and the shadow of something that was once very pretty. Even peppered in rust and dented and lopsided, anyone could imagine how proudly she would have rolled through town back in her glory day. Especially my brother. This was possible. This was real.

Driving down 73rd Avenue he showed off by going fast and when he hit a pothole, the rusty floor under my seat/ the passenger seat cracked and the weight of me and my seat bent the rusty metal beneath me and I dropped a good foot and a half and could hear and feel the road beneath me, scraping the underside of the car and sending sparks about. The car had been charming. Now it was junk.

Tens of thousands of dollars in debt, unemployed and not handy at all, my brother announced to my parents that the student loan check he'd be getting was going to be spent at a body shop where they'd be restoring the old car. His vision was clear, and I'd have loved to have seen it happen. But the cost was way too high, and led my parents to panic. We all agreed that this would ruin his life and that the selfish act would destroy the household. Fighting over nothing would have to wait ... there would be real hell to pay.

The way it was with him was that the more you tried to talk sense to him, the greater his resistance. I relate. But his stubbornness was in a league of it's own. He was determined, and even if our logic sunk in, he couldn't cave in now. He would have his newly restored '62 Rambler. Stay out of his way.

But in just one of a many attempts to save him, and to protect my family, I got in his way.

Late on the night before he was expecting his check to arrive, I took the car keys I'd copied and I drove the green '62 Rambler to a dilapidated waterside levy just outside the gates of Fort Totten in Queens. I drove past the parked cars and parked right next to the water. Brad and Alan met me there in Brad's annoyingly conspicuous Trans-Am Daytona 500 pace car, and we proceeded to get wasted. We waited until the others parked there in cars had finished getting high or laid or whatever, and then there, under the Throgs Neck Bridge I poured blackberry brandy and lighter fluid all over the seats and dashboard and set my big brother's '62 Chevy Impala on fire. The flames flipped, swayed and jumped and I walked numbly and slowly to Brad's hot rod and got in. He and Alan were crapping themselves and screaming at me for actually having done it. Heading for the Clearview Expressway I took one last look at my solution, the heartbreak I'd ignited, my brothers dream there burning orange, green, and blue.

My mother helped Kim report the car stolen the next day while I fought terrible guilt and fear of being found out. Police notified them of the car's discovery and condition the following day. My brother Kim vowed to cut the throat of whomever had stolen his car, should he ever find him. He cried and cried. My parents were upset but mixed due to the unspoken blessing at hand.

My dad sat across from the dining room table from me a few days later and asked if I knew anything about it. I was stoned and still overwhelmed and couldn't hold back my guilty smile. His eyes narrowed and he said "That is NOT OK." But given the insanity that reigned in that family, given how out of touch with his joy and with reality my brother was, and with this expensive and dangerous undertaking just hours away, we both knew that it would have been bad. So I chose a different bad.

I'm really sorry to have caused him so much distress. But if he could ever listen to reason, and now with so much time since that night, I think he'd understand.

Can't say I endorse or recommend spontaneous acts

of destruction. These were extraordinary circumstances, or so I rationalize.

My brother was a searcher. A depressive philosophy major who never made a move without a book or a saxophone in hand and who, through self education or with the help of his misfit associations studied meditation, martial arts, kabbalah, Buddhism and once claimed (to the delight of his junkie friend Nicky and the near demise of our Jewish mother) that he'd accepted Jesus Christ as his lord and savior. He never found love in a partner. The couple of women he spent time with were either prostitutes or still living at home with their moms.

I fantasize that he got the car fixed and took off across country. That he met someone. Someone also running from something and toward they knew not what and that together their search gained steam and that they found something real.

Rusty and broken, perhaps.

But real.

HAIR, 1982 - AGE SEVENTEEN

I'D BULLSHITTED MY way through school and graduated from Jamaica High School halfway through my senior year. I signed up and went to my only choice, Queens College. I shunned the cap and gown, and the opportunity to revel in the achievement I never really cared about. I'd hated school for most of my life. I never even considered walking at graduation. I just wanted to move on, but had absolutely no plan to pursue any of the livelihoods or loves for which I bore an aptitude.

I'd never sought the guidance of a counselor nor had I ever discussed continuing education with any of my teachers, friends, or even my parents. I didn't know that students could apply to more than one college, how to choose a major, or any inkling of what I would do with my life besides being a musician and artist, but I was told from an early age that artists cannot support themselves. It was also drilled into me that the ability to support oneself was essential if one desired a life different than that of my father's—that is, our family's. I could, I supposed, do anything I wanted and all I wanted to do was make and share my art.

This was where "reality" began to wreak havoc on my dreams and—ever the confused and confusing lad—bring me to the unsatisfactory state of achievement in which I find myself today.

Seth Branitz

At the start of senior year, I tried out for the Jamaica High School production of the musical, *Hair*. Clearly, performing was more in alignment with my desires than all this other school shit, so I broke away from the angst-filled routine of keeping my head low, going to some classes and cutting others, and worked up the nerve to audition.

My mouth was dry and quivering as I sang "Sandy" from *Grease* (a capella), and scored the lead roll. Bukowski was heroically cool, misguided, longhaired, and tragic and I related on too many levels to ignore that this was fate. My soul danced and I began to listen to the *Hair* soundtrack with obsessive enthusiasm.

A monkey wrench in this plan arrived a week later, when I was given the opportunity to take an extra humanities class that would permit me to graduate early. The class was seventh period. Rehearsal was seventh period. The choice to let go of this play and to fast track my completely aimless and random future baffles me to this day. I have subsequently walked away from other opportunities and helping hands that might have altered the pace and scope of achieving my real desires, but this particular mistake continues to fuck me up.

The kid who got the part, once I stepped aside, was very popular guy with perfectly blow-dried, dirty blonde hair and a Members Only jacket. While always nice to me, I resented him for being so confident and good at many things. I once walked into the band room and saw him softly playing piano as June Shin sat beside him, hearts in her eyes. Danny appeared to come from money and had a strong, if cocky, stage presence. But he was no Bukowski. He lacked the elements of disenfranchisement and fringe which were daily picks from my natural wardrobe. It rubbed me wrong to have handed him center stage.

I remember nothing rewarding about my last semester but I do remember watching the Jamaica High School production of *Hair*. Seeing Danny perform on opening night was excruciating. My applause. My achievement. My derailing.

He did as fine a job as he could do, and maybe even better than I could have in the stoned, scared and truant condition that was my norm. I like to think I live by the belief that everything happens for a reason and that we're exactly where we're supposed to be and other shit like that, but I see that I don't.

I still wish that I'd done it differently; that I'd given myself the gift of putting myself out there. Somehow, then, my life might have been more rewarding. I might have set the bar higher for taking risks. I might have done a great job instead of quitting. I don't have room any more for decades-old regrets of this sort.

Maybe more importantly, I don't hate Danny Sapperstein any more.

WILD, 1983 - AGE EIGHTEEN

IN THE FIRST of my few semesters of college I was invited to join my high school friend, Leor, and two of his new friends for a few days on the Jersey Shore. I'd played pool with the first, David, and had him pegged as someone who wanted nothing to do with me. Serious and very smart, he'd grown up in Jamaica Estates and graduated from Bronx Science. I laugh now, but I found him threatening. He would loosen up on the drive to Wildwood and become a lifelong friend. The second was Jeff, lanky and affable. I learned almost nothing about him, but Leor thought he'd be fun to have along, and he was partially right.

Conversation on the drive there was moderated by Leor, with very little input from the rest of us. Pulling into Wildwood, the streets were lined with young people, mostly pretty girls with too-tight pants and sweatshirts, butchered to reveal tan, bra-strapped shoulders. The guys were all hyper masculine and ape-like, with baggy pants, gold chains, and shiny hair, we used to call men who subscribed to this style as *"Guido's."*

We entered the motel room, put our bags down, and intuitively proceeded to break the ice by piling onto the beds like puppies, wrestling, head-locking and tumbling to the floor. Now we were good.

Leor was the only one of us with a gift for speaking to girls. We were out of place in a destination known for hooking up and all the girls seems only interested in the slick, scary guys. I had a head of bushy, unkempt hair and wore little more than very tight jeans and cut off t-shirts to show off my daily dumbbell-routine shoulders and long, veiny arms. I was aware of how committed I was to this getup, and wished I could have enjoyed wearing other types of clothes—buttoned shirts, looser jeans, even the balloon-like pants that were popular among young guys at the time, especially the guys that pretty girls seemed to take an interest in.

There was a type of girl who liked guys like me, but not here. They were back in Queens, less pretty and more annoying than my first-choice hotties. They were kind, and kept their crushes a secret until breaking down in a tearful, drunk confession or until finding out that I had another girlfriend. I never knew how to approach the girls I liked, and when they occasionally found their way to me—on *their* terms—I didn't know what hit me. People came to the Jersey Shore to hook up. I didn't know what I was doing there.

A long way from home and with no one to get high with, I got bored very quickly. I had been very isolated back home, dealing coke and black beauties and working a couple of jobs in addition to college. I kept many plates spinning for no particular reason. I guess it looked good from the outside, but I was increasingly irritable and pissed off. I'd thought this few days away would help to keep me from feeling left out, as was always the case.

Leor went off with a girl he'd met, and Dave, Jeff and

I wandered into a bar near the edge of town. It was less crowded than the loud, bustling meat markets and a little easier on our senses. Waiting for my drink at the bar, a guy in his thirties struck up a conversation with me. Very skinny, with a ten o'clock shadow and a cheap Hawaiian-print shirt, he had a nondescript accent and we made small talk. He asked if I knew where he could get some coke. I had brought some extra bags along but hadn't planned to sell any. Talkative and cheerful, he proposed that we go for a walk, saying that the place was crawling with cops. I'd become very tense and was happy to leave, following him through the front door and out to the left, where there was an apartment complex made up of two and three story buildings. He wanted to try the coke and said that if it was good he knew a guy who would buy it all. He said that it would be awful if I were a cop and asked me if I was one. I laughed and said I wasn't and he continued on with his rapid-fire shit-talk, turning behind a building and saying it was just a little further.

After a few steps, he said something else about me being a cop and then turned cold and barked, "*I'm* a cop. Up against the wall." He jammed a hard object into the middle of my back and began a barrage of declarations. "I gonna put a bullet in your head," "You're going to jail," "I'm gonna blow your head off." "I'm gonna fuckin' kill you." He asked me who my source was—who I worked for. I told him I don't have a source, that I get my stuff from a guy named (I made up a name) in Jamaica. He reached around and emptied my pockets, asking where the rest was.

The Trouble With Kim

He kept on pushing the gun deep in between my spine and my shoulder blade. I said that that was all I brought. I thought I heard him cock the gun and asked him to please not kill me. He asked where I was staying. I told him the name of the motel. He read me my name and address off of my license, told me that he now knew where I lived and said he was going to check to see if I had been telling the truth or not. If not, he'd be coming for me. He talked the whole time, intense, deliberate and mean. He directed me to put my hands at my side and told me to begin walking with him back toward town.

He said I was to go back to my motel room and not leave until I heard from him. He walked next to me for a bit, smiling and talking loudly about pretty girls and some other crap. "See you in a little while, *Seeth*," he said, mispronouncing my name but letting me know that he knew who I was. He veered to the left and when I looked toward him he gave me a final glare and repeated, "I know where to find you," and he hurried off into a narrow street of claptrap houses. I walked a little further and saw Dave and Jeff standing outside the bar looking curious.

Approaching them, I said "Keep walking," and tried to contain my tears. They asked where I'd been, what had happened, and if I was ok. I could only manage to say, "Either I'm going to jail or I got ripped off."

The guys said nothing, walked me back to the room to where Leor had just returned, sat on beds and listened to me cry through the bathroom door. I came out, recapped the transaction for them and said I needed to stay in the room until the guy returned. Dave said that the guy was not going to return, that he was leaving town with my drugs, my money and my ID. I sat quietly with the three of them, judged and pitied and still shaking from coming within a finger of my death. They listened. I didn't feel safe.

Hours later, I was still unsure I was allowed to leave, still unclear— as obvious as it was to everyone else—as to whether he had been a cop or not. With no money, ID, or drugs, I wasn't going too far anyway.

There was a knock at the door and Leor let a girl in. He asked us for some privacy and I went for a walk, my senses heightened as I looked into every shop and down every block for my guy. I was equal parts afraid and enraged, ready to avenge. I walked back to our room where Jeff and David were waiting on lawn chairs outside, quiet, and each of us wishing we had Leor's good fortune.

Since high school, Leor had had a confidence few men have. He could talk to anyone, and even girls who I considered out of his league would melt curiously into his charms and often find themselves in his bed. *No fair.* The girl left and returned with a couple of her friends. One of them, a tiny, boy-cut blonde, liked me and we spent the rest of the day and night drinking, talking, kissing—just kissing, I asked for more but she refused—and laughing. I couldn't have asked for a better distraction. She was too drunk to walk back to her room so I carried her on my back. She was fun.

The police, of course, never came for me. I'd like to say that I never again put myself in a dangerous situation, but I did. I still feel the hardness of his gun sticking into my back. I still feel the sheer panic of those long moments when he told me that he was about to take my life.

I've gotten pretty good at forgiving, maybe in part because it's taken a lot for some people to get over my misdeeds and, for the most part, they have. Also, because hating is a burden that I don't have the back for. And because I've seen people turn their lives around and I think everyone is essentially good. This wildwood fucker is an exception. I mean I hope he's no longer doing these cheap robberies and certainly don't want him hurting anyone, but I *hate* him. I don't envision a forgiving embrace, picture him hugging his children, see him smiling or any of the other little exercises I do when I want to forgive someone. *I just hate him.*

While studying martial arts, I often envisioned him and his gun, and have developed muscle memory that might just increase my chances of averting my death, should I ever find myself in a similar scenario. If I ran into him and he was doing much better, clean, respectable, kind, humble, I'd like to say that I'd forgive him, but I'm not sure.

Maybe that means I still have his gun in my back.

Oasis, 1984 - AGE NINETEEN

A TYPICAL BAGEL oven has five shelves that rotate slowly so that you can load or unload one while the others remain suspended, their passengers baking while the baker deals with the shelf at the front. When you press the green button, the shelves resume their cycle, and when you press the red button the next shelf presents itself to get loaded or inspected for done-ness. The shelves rotate up and back, down and forward and each shelf has a certain amount of time in the 475° box before it comes back to the door where it can be dealt with.

In addition to my shifts at the bakery I'd worked at since high school, by nineteen I was an overnight baker at a 24-hour bagel shop on the service road of the Long Island Expressway, "Horace Harding," as it's known locally. The New York Times had celebrated Bagel Oasis as one of the top five bagel places in New York City while I was employed there, a commendation in which I took a good amount of pride.

I'd worked almost as much as I'd partied during high school, and considerably more than I studied. I would sit on the city bus taking me to work after school, and listen with envy to the other kids planning their extracurricular activities, social lives, and mischief.

I was driven to overachieve, to fill the "special" shoes I'd been assigned, and when my interest in school plummeted,

The Trouble With Kim

I just kept on moving in an effort to garner admiration, and distract the realities of my growing problems. I always had a job or two and enjoyed being referred to as "a hard worker." The need to be identified as such has only served to keep me from slowing down long enough to confront my true desires, and formulate a roadmap to their fulfillment. The world has fallen to pieces more than once. Opportunity has flirted with me over drinks, email and frank discussion. I just kept on working.

Both jobs were quick-paced and exciting. I loved being around food and intense heat and I had boundless strength for carrying heavy loads, and energy for long hours.

Even at fifteen I considered myself to be the best dishwasher alive, and I considered the clock as I washed every pot and hotel pan, always approaching the job with the concentration of a protégé and the skill of a ninja. I took this approach in all my work, aiming to be the fastest, strongest, and coolest, at everything from twisting challah to making long-blackened aluminum pans shine silver again.

The principal baker at Bagel Oasis was a tall, scrawny guy a few years older than me, known by the crew as Gay Eddie. He had a chip on his shoulder and—while never overtly unkind—kept a competitive eye on me. Eddie drank a lot and was often late to work, which increased my own workload on those days and led to the bosses' offer to give me a better schedule, which I politely declined because of blind dedication to my other job.

I'd gotten good at working stoned, but noticed myself

dragging if I was hung over, or if I'd recently had cocaine in my system. This was happening more and more often. Exhaustion, social anxiety and debt were replacing the excitement.

I'd done coke with abandon since 11th grade, beginning at a party thrown by one of my high school substitute teachers. She'd filled in for an English teacher for months and was likable and very popular, mostly because she assigned us next to no work.

Ms. Mark was young and Jappy and sounded like Fran Drescher's character on The Nanny.

One Saturday morning she came to the bakery where I worked to say hi, wearing a long mink coat, sweat pants and flip-flops. I was equally impressed by and embarrassed to be seen with her. She and I had gotten close, and she was a fan of my writing and—I suspected—of me. We talked about my struggles with my girlfriend, her aging snowbird parents, drugs, and sex. Curious but not suggesting it, I once asked her how young a partner she'd consider. Her moral code apparently on hand, as she immediately responded that she wouldn't commit statutory rape.

We pined over heavy metal song lyrics and debated the Beatles and the Stones (all Beatles for me at the time), George Carlin and Richard Prior (the latter possessing a hotline to my funny bone), the Electric Company and Zoom (oh...two, one...three, four). She invited me over to listen to music and pulled a large zip-lock bag from the freezer. She sat at her mom's glass coffee table, pushed the bowls of peppermints and jolly ranchers aside, produced long shears, and began to snip huge sections of very green pot into a crystal ashtray and we got more stoned than I'd ever known was possible.

She arranged a party for a handful of us students at her parent's house and she pulled me into a room where we did shotguns and my first lines of coke. I fell immediately in love with the frame of mind it put me in and the confidence with which I walked out of that room drove me to pursue and use cocaine as often as possible.

That's the thing about drugs for me; they did something wonderful. They liberated me, granted me access, balanced my brain. They worked once—or twice. But then when they stopped doing that, I relied on them more and more. Like a bad partner who once showed promise but now presented nothing but grief and degradation, I wouldn't let go.

By this time my grades had plummeted, fueled by my bad relationship and growing darkness at home. I kept working jobs, but I'd lost any remaining focus and despised school. I began smoking pot and drinking first thing in the morning. Once I began using coke daily (smoking it at night) I was cranky, negative and enslaved. I stole money from my parents, conned my dealer, and started selling in order to support my habit. Unable to resist any quantity of the stuff in my proximity, dealing only led me into deeper debt and greater dependence. I anxiously avoided my dealer because I didn't have money to pay him back. I came late to work and burned myself frequently. I started to hate working, and it showed in my performance.

Once, as I had a bagel oven going with two trays loaded and cycling, I went to the bathroom to get a hit. As I walked back to my oven I realized I might have missed my shelf of done bagels. I found that it had run an extra half turn and was now in the rear of the oven. This meant that by the time it got to the front of the oven, that shelf would be burnt, as would the ones behind it. The whole place smelled of burned bread and I couldn't rush the machine. I had to wait, subjecting the shop to my now burning work—a mess, a spectacle—and money in the trash. I soon left that job.

Although I still had a couple of friends I got high with, none were in as deep as I was, and as an evening with one of them would end, so would begin my own escapade. I'd drive on the parkways for hours, head into Manhattan and out to the end of Long Island, or sit, parked on a residential side street and get higher. Or I'd park close to home and walk up and down the length of the streets, covering miles of the grid over a few hours until I was nearly asleep on my feet, and inevitably so far away that I'd curse and cry my way back to my door, and into my bed. There, my body would collapse into dirty sheets but my mind would race with cocaine, amphetamine, and worry.

Hours and miles and dollars on end, my second life had become my new normal and so work, family, friends, and any kind of self care, became hard to fit in, and there came a point where there was no differentiating days from nights—wrong from right, "need" from "need more"—I spent more and more time alone.

The Trouble With Kim

Bosses caught on, and friends got sick of me, and Mom just frowned and the floor kept on dropping out, presenting an array of darkening realities all featuring resignation and quicksand.

I look back on those days with sustained anxiety, much like the default heart-drop when a police car's lights go on behind mine. Always carrying the feeling that I'm a complete fake, about to be found out—about to get fired, about to burn shit.

At the same time, my tendency toward delusions of grandeur remains intact. I'm still the best dishwasher in these parts and can frequently be found in the bouncy-house of my mind, racing soccer moms across the Tappan Zee Bridge and winning televised dishwashing contests. I was a little less distracted, a lot less destructive.

Ever the ninja—ever the sham.

JOHNNY, 1983 - AGE EIGHTEEN

JOHNNY WAS ALWAYS smiling. He was flabby and had shiny black hair, long and parted in the middle. His nose was nice, long and sloped up into a point. He was a year younger than me, soft and effeminate, always with pretty girls I expect he wasn't having sex with.

I'd recently started hanging out on the other side of an adjoining housing development called Electchester, with children of white electricians, builders and carpenters. There were a number of kids from the neighborhood beyond, who lived in private houses. Until then, I'd remained closer to the nest of the heavily integrated federal housing project called Pomonok, where I grew up.

There was some perceptible difference in quality of life once we crossed Parsons Boulevard, and although no one ever told us that they were in any way better off than us, *I* thought so. Their buildings and sidewalks were in better shape, and their streets and parking lots hosted cars from the current decade.

Johnny and these other new kids were zoned for different high schools and some went to Catholic school. I was very much an outsider, having not grown up with them—living a good half mile away—and being Jewish. Our common ground was getting high at the park on 168th Street, and our individual and collective desires to avoid going home. There was no cozy feeling among these guys. I didn't know any of them as well as they knew each other. They'd grown up together. I didn't go to their houses, and they never came to Pomonok. I didn't understand Ed Meyer's sense of humor, and never figured out if the others were laughing *at* his jokes or *with* him. I was afraid of Pete Disiani's angry rants about his asshole brother and his fucking girlfriend. And while Paulie Caminetti and I shared a genuine affection for one another, we had little to say unless we were fucked up. I don't think that either of us was impressed with the other.

If I wasn't being validated, at least they didn't reject me. If they didn't know much about me, then they couldn't hold much against me. I needed a respite from the gripping darkness that was my family dynamic. There was endless fighting, blaming, walking on eggshells, depression, and guilt trips. I carried my shame over falling from the high graces of my family and my teachers. I had become more concerned with escaping my pain than with anything else, and I was consumed by that pursuit.

One afternoon I walked up the block and saw a sweet old lady I knew walking toward me. Mrs. Meyer would always smile, at me and ask how I was, and say how tall I was getting. She, like several of the elderly neighbors who had watched me grow, helped me to feel good being me. On this day however, she crossed the street to walk on the other side and to avoid the seedy, longhaired teen with black leather and torn jeans that I'd become. I felt as if I'd been sentenced to a harsh penalty for a crime I'd been falsely accused of. I was ashamed, angry and confused.

Around the same time, I drove up behind my friend Jimmy Lang's house, and honked the horn for him to come down. I was met by his mother, who stuck her head out the window to see who was calling. I felt guilty knowing I was there to exchange drugs, but since we'd had a cordial relationship up until then I thought I hid it well. Jimmy called me later that night to say that his mom didn't want me coming around anymore. I was devastated.

My bad choices had been compounding more quickly than we were growing up. And now I found solace in this built-in community of kids who didn't know I was a problem, and who shared similar drugging prowess. We'd hang out in the park late into winter nights, smoking weed, washing pills down with chugs of Southern Comfort and Lancers, and making believe that there was no school tomorrow. No mothers waiting up worried. No hangovers imminent.

Johnny was the first person I ever saw drink so much that he couldn't get up, vomit all over his lap, take another swig from the bottle, and throw up again. He smiled all the while and I liked him. He was nice to me and bought coke a few times then convinced me to front him some, promising to pay me by the end of that weekend.

He was very sweet and boyish, always making eye contact, smiling and gentle. This was a far cry from my dealings with most other kids, some of whom were seedy, and made me worry about getting us caught or robbing me. Others were in the anxious grips of a habit, and this reminded me that I was doing something wrong. I liked

The Trouble With Kim

Johnny and thought it would be good for both of us if he could sell some coke now and then, so I fronted him a quantity worth several hundred dollars.

I, myself, was already in debt to my dealer friend, Carlos, from Jamaica High School who had recently been arrested right there in the auditorium during assembly, but was back in school now using a different first name and selling more than ever. He had his Colombian family connections, and crazy pitches about how this batch had been dropped from a helicopter and retrieved on the runway at Flushing airport, or that batch had been smuggled in the heads of Cabbage Patch dolls. He was a born salesman and I thought we were friends, but now I owed him money and his demeanor had changed.

It was highly inconvenient that Johnny began to avoid me. I would run down to the park and near his house looking for him, and he seemed to have just disappeared. I was sure it was just bad timing as I couldn't accept that he'd turned on me, whether inspired by bad intentions or desperation. After a few days of no contact, I arrived at the park and Paulie told me that Johnny said nasty things about me, and that he would never pay me. All practical matters aside, this hurt. I thought we had an understanding. I thought I was OK by him. I was being pressured about the money I myself owed for merchandise, most of which I'd personally consumed. Johnny continued to duck me as I ducked my guy, and I was digging an ever-deepening hole.

One afternoon, desperate to get some of my own debt paid off, I went to the park where someone told me Johnny had just left after laughing about his successful avoidance, and I went to the corner of 65th Avenue, turned left—up the steep hill that always left me winded—walked three blocks and turned right. My breathing was very fast. and I felt hot as I rehearsed my plea. I would first collect my money, and then call him any number of names, leave him remorseful. He'd fear and respect me from there forward. I'd go directly to pay some of my debt, get high and call the day a success.

I got to the little Archie Bunker colonial, stepped slowly up the front stoop and rang the bell. I heard shuffling and through the screen door I saw the frowning face of Johnny's mother. She seemed to have been expecting trouble. After a few seconds of looking at one another I asked if Johnny was home. She hesitated then called to him. He popped out from right behind her where he'd been hiding and said, "What do you want?" I said that I needed the money he owed me. He denied that he did. He was frowning and for the first time, looked evil to me. I hadn't planned for this resistance.

I said, "Mrs. Byrum, your son is drug addict, and a dealer and a liar, and he's stealing from me." Johnny stepped right up to the screened door and growled at me. "You FUCK! I'll never give you your money."

I turned my body to walk away, already defeated and feeling horrible for what I'd done to his mother, but rage overcame me and I spun back around and punched right through the screen. He fell back into his mothers arms, mouth full of blood, screen door torn from the frame and dangling. They both looked at me in horror, all of us equally surprised by the attack.

I sprung down the steps and strode long-legged down the street, swinging my arms and panting audibly. I broke into a trot, then a run into Electchester and across to the far side where the woods were. I became aware of the pain in my hand as skin peeled away from my knuckles every time they brushed on my pant leg. I fell with my back to a tree and cried hard when an inspection of my hand bore evidence of the damage I'd inflicted. I wanted to go back, to make the past ten minutes go away and for Johnny's smile to be restored. For the scars that I still wear on my hand to have been a nightmare borne of aggressive fantasy. To be free of this compulsion to always be high, and to become a likable, sweet and gifted boy once again. *Or to die.*

But I did not get what I wanted and I didn't see Johnny any more. Shameful and humiliated, I stopped going to that park, only occasionally dealing with—*or to*—some of those kids but only if they came to the near edge of Electchester, close to where I lived. Johnny and I never crossed paths, what with the distance, and him avoiding me.

I flopped around in the typhoon of my own addiction for years, and separated myself from those that cared but did not know how to help, and when help presented itself, I scoffed. I grew accustomed to knowing that there were people in the world to whom I was trouble. *Even evil.*

Years later, when I was clean, I again approached the emergency room entrance to Booth Memorial Hospital to visit my mom, who'd had a seizure. I came face to face with

Johnny. He was in hospital attire and I assumed that he was an orderly or a technician, and I was glad. It took little effort to put out my hand and he didn't hesitate to take it and we shook like men do, and then we kept going. His smile was beautiful and his teeth, intact.

The moment he was out of sight I wished I had told him how sorry I was. How he didn't deserve to be hated and shamed and attacked, and how I was wrong, and how I wish I could have done it differently. I wished I'd have told him how I'd regretted my actions immediately, and how it had stayed with me ever since. I also wished he'd have forgiven me so I could begin to forgive myself.

About a third of the way down on a long but narrowing list of people with whom I've been attempting to make things right, lies the name Johnny Byrum. Not long ago I tried to contact him and learned that he died. I'm not sure how he met his fate but way too young, I think. And I'm sadder than I would have expected to be.

There are fuck-ups I'll never live down, the hardest part of which is knowing that I might leave behind a legacy of misdeeds, if even for one person (though there are others). Thinking back on that handshake outside the hospital I take solace in my hope that our civilized conduct bore an implied mutual forgiveness.

That is, maybe he forgave me.

And hopefully himself.

I'm working on the rest.

CLEARVIEW, 1984 - AGE NINETEEN

I WAS DRIVING late one night, my eyes tightly closed, south toward Jamaica on the Clearview Expressway. I was completely devoid of hope, and needing a break from the constant nagging darkness that enveloped my life. I made deals with myself and with God. I would lie in the tub and hold my breath until I passed out. If I drowned, so be it.

Or I'd do more drugs than a crowd of guys my size, and when I could barely move, I'd take some more—not quite suicide, not really a party.

Or I'd close my eyes while driving. This night I entered the middle lane and vowed to close my eyes and continue driving for a count of ten. I opened them to find that I was only slightly out of my lane. Then twenty. I opened them to find myself in the next lane but still pretty straight.

Then fifty. Whatever would happen would happen.

The car rumbled over the curb onto the dirt and grass and I opened my eyes in time to avoid the stone overpass wall. I swerved sideways and the car jumped up on the two passenger-side wheels, then dropped back down with a most jarring thud. I put the car in park and saw how close I had come to what could have been the end of my suffering, to the end of my underachieving, worrying my parents, and alienating my remaining friends. I saw the faces of the innocent whose lives I could have ended or ruined, in thinking only of myself.

I also considered the songs, the stories scribbled there in several black-and-white marble notebooks, barely legible to even me, lacking the melody and music that only I knew. And I thought about how if I could just stop getting high all the time, how I might have a chance to strum them out on my beat up Japanese Strat and sing them for people. Maybe someone would listen. Maybe I'd be proud.

I realized that I had used all of my drugs, and that I needed to get to my dealer (though I owed him money) or to Tommy, (who was growing paranoid and thought I'd sent the cops his way—I *hadn't),* or to my Jamaica Ave. cop-spot for more.

And then the light came on. Not the light of a spirit or of an awakening, and not the one that had been on and off for months, that tells me the engine is in jeopardy of seizing if I don't give it attention soon (I never did and the engine finally seized). But now the one next to it that says that fuel is low, and that if you don't add some gas soon you'll be out of luck.

And then I struck myself in the face. *Hard.* My eye stung, and I could not see through it, but sat there and pounded myself. Cars whizzed by and shook mine and I kept on hitting myself, and without looking over my left shoulder, I slammed it into drive and floored it, the tires spun in the dirt and finally caught, and I lunged back into my seat and onto the expressway. I struck myself again. I've hit people before, and this was not that hard, because I was projecting the force back toward myself and didn't have the benefit of torque or of extending my arm, I thought. So I leaned back to the headrest and swung it forward, hard, into the steering wheel.

I was dizzy and nauseous, and I hit my head a few more times. I was sweating and hyperventilating until I was drenched in sweat. Until finally, the pain was gone. How I drove on I don't know.

I really wanted to die.

But I really wanted to live.

The songs, I think, were the thing I most treasured. Maybe they were even why I'd been born. I felt an obligation to deliver this gift I had, but had no access to the confidence—not to mention the clarity—to organize a plan; and if I had, no one would have listened to a fuck-up like me anyway. And this fucking cocaine I knew I should never have started smoking, and Mom's Valium and cheap whiskey which was the only way I could sleep, and whether it was my art or my fix, I lived torn between what I needed and what I lacked. I couldn't keep up anymore.

My parents who needed me; Kim, whose own addiction had now surpassed his mental illness, and was killing all three of them. My big brother was quickly becoming my little brother. And Danielle, the sweetest, most understanding and gullible girl, who believed I was good and was my only escape from the fall, and who I was more and more frequently leaving too soon because *I had to go!*

Go to the gym, to practice, to work, or to sleep. "My head is pounding," I'd say. (It always was). And she, disappointed but sweetly allowing me to go do the thing. But the only thing I did was nothing. I stalked and consumed my drugs and then hung out alone to let the high sink in, or to die. I drove for hours, using it all, and then trying to get more.

As with so many of these nights, I don't know how I managed to get high and to get home. Maybe I stopped and slept in the car on a side street in Bayside, windows cracked so they wouldn't fog and attract a patrolling cop. Maybe I ended up at Carl's house, or one of my other sources, stayed up all night partying, and went straight to work in the morning. Maybe I snuck into Danielle's garage and lay on the cushion-less lounge chair, rolled up in a ball shivering and crying for what felt like forever until the sun came up and my disbelief compounded, and my hatred bred hatred, bred hatred. Maybe I waited at Kissena Park, across from the dudes who sold bags of most anything from the bench inside the playground. Waited for them to finally leave and then maybe this was one of the nights I'd crawled around on the ground under the benches in the dark, in broken glass and loogies, looking for a bag or a foil or a coke-laced joint or—lowest on the score list— some crumpled up money that had missed a wasted dealers pocket and gone unnoticed under the broken lamppost light. Sometimes I went there first thing in the morning if I'd been out all night long, or before work if I could get up a few minutes early, and that would save me the added challenge of darkness. Getting a jump on my day's vital to-do list.

The Trouble With Kim

It hurt like hell to lie down, my big face pouring off of my head, my one eye mostly closed and full of broken blood vessels. This marked a new low, but not the last.

Here's the story others heard: A guy cut me off on the Clearview. He was raging, swerving and literally ran me off the road and forced my car to a stop. He got out of his car and ran to mine, opened my door, pulled me out and beat me. He was huge, but I somehow subdued him and messed him up pretty bad, walking to my car and driving off, but not without taking a few shots to the head. This garnered sympathy and admiration I desperately needed, while avoiding (as was my way) any contest of my lifestyle. Instead of the fuck-up, I was the hero for the time it took for these wounds to heal.

And it wasn't truly a lie. Some inebriated and reckless asshole HAD run me off the road. And then in a fit of rage I HAD been assaulted and struck over and over, until said asshole had been subdued, and I was able to escape by driving off to relative safety.

This is how I was able—just barely—to live with myself and with the choices I made or which were made for me by default. It's how I got to abuse, cheat, thieve, lie, hurt, crash and burn. I kept to myself because there was no one in the world who was remotely as fucked up as I was, no one who would understand and no one who could help.

Except of course for those homeless, murderous, clinically disabled show-offs who were luckily excused responsibility for their condition, except to the extent that it allowed them to coast through life with a different set of rules, or without any at all. Crazy people had a license to misbehave and to self-destruct. Now I related to them and was sure that they understood me, except that I was not crazy. I was merely despicable.

Everyone made me sick and no one could help.

These are the brand of lies I keep a close look out for today, all these years later, as I still lie alone with my thoughts. They would make me run each time there was a threat of change, or a hint of sameness, and would tell me that there's something awfully wrong with what I am, that I'm not well suited for surviving in this place—that I *must* achieve more, and that there's no chance I can. That I'm not welcome, and I had better just end it now before life falls to bits once again.

But there have been different versions of me. There's one that has learned to consider before reacting, and is therefore equipped not only to manage horrible turns of events, but who also finds a reason to tolerate, if not respect—even adore—every rung on this splintering ladder called mortality.

This shit isn't easy.

PAT DOWN, 1985 – AGE TWENTY

THE GUY WHO sold weed through the slot in the green door next to the bodega wasn't there. I asked a seedy looking kid on the corner about him.

"Where's Huggy Bear?"

"Huggy-Bear in jail."

This guy, glad to take the business from his indisposed associate reached his hand out to me and then opened it to reveal the cellophane envelope with small, white rocks. I'd been badly hooked on coke on-and-off for years, and at the moment was managing myself with a variety of pills, weed, and drink. Crack was something I hadn't yet tried, and I saw what it was doing to people. Ira Ross had just told me that he was so hooked that he was going to hit an old lady on the head for her money. Kenny from high school and his brother had robbed a lady and accidentally killed her. I feared, more than I hated, how my life was going, and had kept a safe distance from this particular poison, so when I found myself in this transaction, money in one hand and crack being passed into my other, I knew that I was in danger.

An uncontrollable fury overtook me and I said, too loudly, "Not fuckin' *crack!*" He said, "*ooooohhhh*, you want *weeeeed*," and told me that he'd take me to where it was.

I followed the kid to a brick apartment building and he pointed up to the front door and kept walking to the

131

next corner, watching shadily over his shoulder. I walked up the brick stoop, pulled the heavy front door open and entered the lobby. There were two women sitting on the steps and one standing near them, leaning against the wall of mailboxes. The sound of children running and laughing echoed from a hallway above. Doors opened and closed. Phones rang through closed, metal doors. One of the women was standing on the third or fourth step up, arms folded and frowning. She leaned down to me and said, "May I help you?" On the spot and out of place, I now suspected I'd walked into the wrong group of strangers and thought better of asking them for drugs. I muttered something about James telling me I could find what I needed in this building. The seated woman barked, "Who the fuck James?"

I began to say that I was in the wrong place and turned to leave when the first woman asked if I was a cop. I said that I wasn't and she said that, legally, I had to tell them if I was. Realizing the irony of them suspecting me to be a cop, I again assured them, and the standing woman said that she'd check. "Face the wall." I turned to the mailboxes and she patted me down, gesturing for my arms to be raised. She felt around for a gun or a badge, down the front of my torso, bent to feel my ankles and worked her way up and then ran her hands across the front of my pants, the three of them breaking into laughter as she said, "I like this!" She felt around the back, gave my ass a little squeeze, playing to her audience who were now screaming in hysterics. I objected flirtatiously, not knowing what else to do.

I copped my dime bag and got the fuck out.

JERRY, 1982 - AGE SIXTEEN

DURING HIGH SCHOOL I did weekend shifts at a sweater warehouse where my girlfriend, Donna, had worked for years. The place was dark and smelled like yeast, and we sometimes wore masks so as not to get sick from all the mold, and the wool, cotton, and polyester dust. Her family was oddly enmeshed with the owners.

Donna's sister would pick up sweaters at a mill and deliver them to their mother. Donna's Polish immigrant mother—who was four foot something, round, and spoke almost no English—would sew designer labels into them so they could be sold as designer sweaters. Size labels were pinned on, and if the order called for more of a certain garment in a size that we did not have, we would just pin on the label of the desired size. Donna's sister, Barbara, was fifteen years older than we were, and she worked there as a manager. She and Donna were both tall and slender—with what I'd heard women on daytime talk shows call "excellent bone structure"—and green-blue eyes. Barbara, or Basia ("Basha") wore thick square red-framed glasses that seemed to temper her conventional beauty. She was the bosses' left hand, very sharp, and seemed to know everything about Hillside Wholesalers, perhaps even more than Jerry did. She sometimes traveled with Jerry on business trips.

Hillside Wholesalers was owned by Harold and Jerry. Upon my initial interrogation, Jerry Rosenzweig discovered that he was a childhood friend of my father's kid brother, and knew my dad and his whole family. This was exciting to me and when I told my dad, he remembered Jerry as a rambunctious, short-fused kid. After a few weeks of relaying messages back and forth between them, my dad took a ride to Queens Village to visit with Jerry. They immediately hit it off. I enjoyed seeing Dad laugh, and it was fun hearing Jerry corroborate some of the East Side fables I'd heard my dad tell for so long.

Jerry was seedy. He was tall and chubby and he twisted and bucked when he walked because of a bad hip. I saw him as more of a cowboy than a merchant. His office was a corner of the shop, always littered with random items that had fallen off a truck: radar detectors, VCR's, Members-Only jackets, diamonds; what hair he had was frizzy, unkempt and riddled with dandruff. He had a bushy mustache that nearly covered his stubby, grey teeth, through which he was always grinning. He gazed without blinking through his bulging, black eyes and I always felt afraid to look away, but wasn't crazy about looking directly at him either.

He was an epileptic diabetic, a couple of side effects of which were that he had no sense of taste, and that his body was resistant to anesthesia and could not be numbed. So his frequent visits to the dentist were occasion for great deals of pain. He claimed to be awake for the whole procedure, whatever it was this time. When I asked if it hurt, he answered, "Shit yeah, it hurt!!"

Jerry was tough, but kind.

The Trouble With Kim

My father told me he had killed somebody.

A man had owed him money and he committed premeditated murder for which he'd done hard time. After his release, he resumed being a businessman and made millions.

I knew far less about his partner, Harold. Harold was grossly obese, with a voice like Kermit the Frog. When he caught Donna and me fooling around while perusing the vast porn mag collection we'd discovered under an old pinball machine in the basement, he gave us a lecture on how desperate these girls are and how they are all on drugs and had no self esteem, and some other shit we just could not believe he was saying. We made no apologies, nor did he ask us to keep our hands off, though the request was implied and we all just wanted to get the fuck out of there. I had a stack of them already crammed into my backpack so I never needed his pile again.

Harold had always been the bookkeeper, and when he'd had emergency back surgery and was out for a while recuperating, Jerry noticed some inconsistencies in accounting. Harold returned to begin putting in a few hours of work, and in the first five minutes back, Jerry opened the books and pointed to a page that had a few entries that he had highlighted. Harold sat quietly for a few long moments then stood, took his coat off the back of his chair, calmly put it on and left. Jerry claimed never to have heard from him again. I was pretty sure that Harold was a dead man, but heard nothing to verify that suspicion.

Knowing my family's dire financial situation, Jerry

offered to help. He would consign sweaters that were "seconds" to my dad. Mom would mend them if they had a hole or a thread-pull, and spot-clean any visible stains. The fact was that most of them were perfect. My parents would then sell them at flea markets and they would split the proceeds.

My parents surprised me by agreeing to what would be their first-and-only attempt at industry. Within weeks, my mom had rented space at the weekly St. Nicholas of Tolentine flea market on the border of Jamaica and Flushing, and had purchased two folding tables. They packed up the like-new sweaters, a couple of folding chairs and a shoebox full of fives and singles, drove the mile to the huge church parking lot, schlepped the goods to their spot and quickly learned the tricks of the trade, which included the optimal time to arrive (no later than. 6:30 am or else the high traffic sites were taken), when to decide whether to cancel or not (listening to weather forecasts and crossing fingers), how to tactfully deal with competition (smile at them but tell customers made-up stories about how they sourced their goods) and knowing when to say no to a low offer. Mom would do this if the customer rubbed her the wrong way. She turned down a lot of lowball offers. Good for her, I thought.

Mom would eventually bring thermoses of soup and coffee and a box of saltines so Dad wouldn't get too hungry and ruin the day. And although the vendors were all protected and protective, and no tight bonds were formed, my parents clearly enjoyed this new lot. They resisted spending their earnings on treasure-junk at adjoining tables and they faithfully stashed money away into a white envelope in a manila envelope in a shoebox in Mom's sock and hose drawer.

Dad would stop in every few weeks to pick up merchandise from Jerry, and to pay him for goods sold. After a few times Jerry said to hold on to it, that Dad didn't owe him for that last batch. He continued to give my parents sweaters to sell but soon altogether stopped accepting payment. Dad always offered, but Jerry would just wave his hand or change the subject. I worried about possible ulterior motives but soon accepted this routine as a quiet act of charity and I was grateful for it, impressed with Jerry's kindness, but also with my parents' choice to receive help in this fashion. It showed me that they thought they deserved something good, that they were willing to live in something other than victimization, gloom, and doom. My parents were otherwise unemployed and it was this money that enabled them to eat out a couple of times a week, grab a movie now and then and even to throw me a few bucks when I needed it.

Donna and I fought all the time, but immaturity and low self-esteem kept us from breaking up sooner. We had nothing in common, apart from mutual affection and a bond built in isolation. Once, when I hadn't come over in a week or more, she fooled around with a kid in the neighborhood. She first told me that something had happened over the phone, but when I confronted her, drunkenly, outside her house at close to midnight on a school night, she admitted that she'd not only hung out with him a few times, but that she liked him and that they'd had sex. I rode my brothers blue Raleigh ten speed bike up and down the dark, tree-lined streets screaming, "*Kenny Brewer*! Get the fuck *out* here!" I'd never met the kid, but was about as close to murder as I'd ever come. My explosion left me defeated and exhausted, vision obstructed by tears, and I walked the bike most of the uphill slog home.

Despite those troubles, Jerry remained in my family's lives for a while. My dad and he began to run out of memories to recount, and the novelty wore thin. After a winter break from the flea markets my parents were too sick to continue.

My dad told me that Jerry had long been sleeping with Donna's sister, and this thought bothered me more than I could understand. Donna and I had been a great disappointment and now whatever solid recollections of that period I still had were blemished. I was confused by the pairing of these two married adults and the thought of it just made the world a little uglier.

I recently gave away the last of the sweaters I'd gotten from Jerry thirty years ago, black cable-knit, stretched and holey.

When I lay in bed at night I've got this habit of imagining that I'm black, on a bed of straw in 1850 Mississippi, or Jewish on a plank in 1939 Lichtenburg, or alone on a cot, infected, 1986, Christopher Street. And I feel undeserving of my health, my warm bed and my freedom. I relate to their impending doom and their heart's desires, and I get sad and sometimes I cry, and somehow this is how I find my way to compassion, and sometimes to gratitude. Maybe it's just a way to punish myself with guilt.

And always as I lay under the dentist's light getting prodded and drilled, I think about Jerry, feeling everything and imagine that I'm that lonely, seedy, generous, wonderful and tough motherfucker. And I tighten up and grin right through the pain.

COUCH, 1987 - AGE TWENTY-TWO

MY BASEMENT APARTMENT on Meacham Avenue was a moldy studio with ceilings so low that I banged my elbow into the drop ceiling every time I put on my Right Guard roll on deodorant. I got good at making it from my bed into the bathroom to throw up in just four steps.

I could turn the couch so that it was only five feet from the kitchen sink, over which I smoked coke nightly. I'd light up and inhale as long and as deeply as I could, drop the paraphernalia—which would self-extinguish—into the sink, step backwards and fall into the welcoming fluff of my dirty old, curb-gotten couch. I'd hold my breath for as long as possible, and then I'd exhale very slowly—the dose too precious to waste—many times I passed out holding off the next breath. The couch was my cradle and I was safe.

For a half second, for the very early part of the inhale, it was bliss.

Then all I could think about was more.

CHEESE, 1986 - AGE TWENTY-ONE

I ONCE VENTURED to buy a famous cheese shop in one of the richest towns in the world. I'd dropped out of college in a cloud of smoke and incompletes, and was happy for a break from the long run of finger-to-shoulder burns that I was collecting while coked out and reaching into bagel ovens on graveyard shifts.

I thought that Jerry's partnership—the same Jerry who owned the sweater company and who helped my parents out by giving them sweater seconds to sell at flea markets—in the purchase of Cheese of the World in Great Neck was going to be my ticket out of the lower class. His support would make up for the complete void my father's incompetence had created. His resources would allow me to correct the course my poverty-mentality had set my family on for generations. I could dig myself out of debt. I could be really good at something and my friends could write me back in. I could get rich fast and sell the business, make demos, get discovered, tour, and take the world by storm. I could afford my drugs and if things got bad again I'd be able to afford rehab. I could help my parents out and set my brother up. I could be somebody. My troubles would be over.

My naïveté bordered on delusional.

The owner of the shop, Leslie, was the son-in-law of the founder, who had died long ago. He was very tall with wavy, unkempt hair and a reassuring smile on his pockmarked face. The widow, Ruthie, advancing in age and her senses dulling, was there almost every day. Equal parts blue-haired deputy and shuffling mascot, many customers would allow only her to serve them and she spent a part of each shift contradicting, correcting, and schooling the new boss, the other clerks, and me. I never figured out if I liked her or not.

In the beginning I found it hard to stomach the pungent aroma rising from the seventy or so cheeses—they had apparently once carried over one hundred and thirty— that wafted into every inch of the space, my clothes, skin and hair. But just as had happened after years in bakeries where I loved every aroma produced, I eventually became desensitized to the smell.

Prior to working there I could not bear to consider eating any smelly, aged cheeses, and was repulsed by the mere sight of soft ripening varieties such as Camembert. Before long I became skilled at wire-cutting huge wheels of cheese with precision, could cut a custom wedge to within five one hundredths of a pound by eye, and had acquired a taste for most of the inventory, a working knowledge of the rest.

I sat with Leslie, the cheese man, with whom I'd now become friends, and took down the pertinent business information. I brought the "books" and a copy of the lease to Jerry and we talked about the shop, it's history, the flow, the clientele, and my thoughts on its potential. I talked about the neighborhood and what I'd learned when visiting other cheese stores or "gourmet shops," all the while sure that I had it in the bag, and looking forward to my life being saved. He asked few questions and always looked at me long and unblinkingly with an intensity I learned to identify as somewhere between deeply affectionate and psychotic. He was oversized and disheveled, but composed and cocky. I admired Jerry and thought of him as family, although he always scared me.

He saw right through me, and knew that my drug habit had worsened. He spared me the shame of a confrontation, and said that the numbers didn't add up. He was sorry, but it was not a moneymaking situation and so he withdrew his willingness to invest. Several times he looked me in the eye and said, "Let me know if you or your family need any help," which simply baffled me as here he was leaving me flat on my face.

I asked Sal, a coke dealer I knew, if he was interested in partnering with me on the purchase of the business. He knew what a hard worker I was and showed some interest. He got us on a conference call with a friend of his named Dave, whom he thought might help me out. A fast and flowery talker, Dave kept reiterating the details of the deal and made light of my inability to find a family member to back me. "You mean to tell me you're *Jewish* and no one in your family has money to put you into business?!"

The truth is that Jerry saved me from far greater pain, not to mention saving himself. Up to that point, my train-wrecks had not featured great sums of money. So once I was able to own all the ways in which I had failed my friends, my employers, my family, and my own vision, I was able to forgive Jerry. He knew the deal.

At the time though, I was devastated.

I stayed on working for Leslie and the trade that I had been excited to learn now became a job, drudgery, and I was once again stuck. Again I wished I'd had a different father and had stayed in college. And again I fell to a new low, saw no way out and talked to no one about it.

Danielle was my girlfriend and it was her brother, John, who had originally planted the seed by letting me know that the place was for sale. He'd worked for Leslie for a few years, and was about to leave after a disagreement over the handling of money while managing.

He and I used to buy pot from a hairdresser in town on Fridays, and once when I was headed to my parents for a visit, he told me that I had to go there straight. He yelled that I shouldn't be getting stoned to see my parents. I knew that of all the occasions where it was in my best interest to be stoned, doing so before visiting my parents topped the list.

John went on to become a private investigator of some repute and I always cared for him, even after Danielle and I had broken up.

I called in sick as often as I could, and avoided Danielle and my friends during the months after Jerry walked away. I fell months behind on my rent, and avoided my landlord by parking blocks away, sneaking into my moldy basement apartment late at night.

The Trouble With Kim

On one of these late nights I got to the door only to find that I couldn't locate my apartment key. Unable to face my landlord without past-due rent in hand, I kneeled at one of the basement windows, which measured approximately three feet wide and eighteen inches high. Using a screwdriver I was able to break and remove the screen and then bend the aluminum window frame and slide the window-lock open. Its hinge was at the bottom and it opened out and lay flat in the small window box. Minutes passed while I strategized possible entry options; feet first or head first?

Belly down or belly up?

The window being at the very top of the apartment wall and perpendicular to the ceiling of my apartment, I decided on feet first, on my back. I spread the weight of my bony person over the window frame, careful to avoid laying on the pane of glass beneath me. I shimmied inch-by-inch, and made good progress until I began to fatigue with my legs dangling into the dark apartment, my nose inches from the top of the window box and no clear way to proceed or retreat. A cramp radiated from my hips to my neck, and I was stuck. I could feel the flat window on my protruding spine, and was afraid of it breaking and severing my spine, leaving me paralyzed and bleeding. I resolved to scream and hope for help from the guy who lived in the street level apartment above. He'd be able to grab my hands and slide me out and then I could approach my descent into the basement with a fresh approach, maybe even ask him to lower me to assure a safer landing.

Then the glass crushed beneath me. Already trapped, I

145

was now being punished and nothing I did could alleviate the sharp mess from pinching and poking into my back. I escaped with little more than a few cuts. My window got fixed, I found my key and I stepped on tiny shards of glass many times for months to come.

I was oblivious to the effect my behavior was having on my friends. I'd detached so thoroughly, that when Danielle told me about her upcoming graduation day from her Masters program, I treated it as optional and told her I would try. Then, despite the years of school I'd seen her through, I didn't go.

Danielle had been a serious girlfriend. At first coworkers at the bakery, we began hanging out when Donna and I were breaking up. She was fun loving and kind, and we fell easily into one another's groups of friends. Her big Italian family took me in, and mine were very pleased having mild mannered Danielle replace Donna, with whom I'd fight over the phone, and who's neighborhood I'd disappear into for days without checking in.

She and I got high together at first, but she pulled back and began to disapprove of the frequency and quantities that I was using. When she found out I was dealing, she was frightened and asked me to stop. I told her I would. She wanted to believe me. I hid my drug use and so saw less and less of her.

It was during this dark period, after Jerry pulled out, that I had two minor but significant breakdowns.

The first occurred when Jay and I got into a cold car and

The Trouble With Kim

I insisted on blowing the heater immediately in order to circulate the air in my car—which I deemed unbreathable from all the smoke, ash and filth that had been it's regular state for years—but he thought it best to let the engine heat up first for a more efficient use of the heater. We went back and forth a few times, each flicking the heat lever our preferred way and raising our voices until I screamed at him, kept screaming, and then began crying uncontrollably. He didn't know what to do. Through my sobs, my face buried in my hands against the steering wheel, I could hear him murmuring, "C'mon, man. It's ok. C'mon, Seth." When I caught my breath, I apologized and he asked if I was ok, to which I said I was, that I was just going through a lot. This seemed to satisfy him, although I could feel him watching me as I drove him home.

The next was when I finally cried to Danielle about my deep, helpless depressed state and how my life was over. I told her that I know there is more for me but that nothing goes my way and now I was going to die before I get a chance to realize my potential. She empathized powerfully and told me it would be ok.

In both cases I scared the loved ones present and in both cases, they reported to each other. There was no clear intervention, but I believe the meeting of their kind hearts and good minds created some kind of a space for me to hear Danielle when she told me I needed help. She was the first.

She told me that a social-work student friend of hers recommended Alcoholics Anonymous. I thought this an inappropriate course of action, as I was still sure that my consumption and my circumstances were unique. The seed was planted and I resolved to go to a meeting and to bare my soul. Terrified and alone, I procrastinated for months more—this, after years of already admitting to myself that I was trapped. AA—it turned out—was not for me, what with a rule that discouraged sharing about drugs in favor of alcohol,* and the fact that the average attendee was a middle aged or older man.

At my first meeting, the senior citizen who was qualifying at the beginning of the meeting asked a young brunette in the front row to get him a black coffee, calling her, "Blondie," and failing to say please or thank you. A guy approached me after the meeting and there told me of the existence of Narcotics Anonymous, saying that it would be more appropriate for me to go there.

My first NA meeting was in a church near the railroad in Valley Stream, NY. As I approached the door, I was greeted by a towering black man I'd never seen before. He opened his arms, and for a second I tried to compute where I knew him from, what he wanted, and how to escape what could have been danger. Before I could answer these questions, his long arms were around me and I was in tears, my face pressed against his chest. He swayed me side to side and kept on saying, "Welcome." His name was Tree Rob. I don't remember the rest of the meeting, expect that I was handed a meeting list on the back of which a dozen or so men had written their first names and phone numbers.

I went to a few meetings, and after a week or so, I

stopped using and stayed stopped. I obsessed on the program's suggestions and avoided anyone I'd gotten high with. I began to feel some hope and put on a few pounds (I was 6' and 147 lbs. when I got clean. Only months later I tipped 200 lbs.)

A couple of months into my recovery, Danielle, my girlfriend of five years, broke up with me saying that I'd changed into someone different. The irony was as painful as the loss.

Once I'd gotten over the initial painful aftermath of the cheese shop, I wanted to ring Jerry up to thank him and to let him know that while I wasn't exactly doing well, I was clean. I wanted him to know that I understood his choice and that it was the right one. His phone numbers didn't work and I know nothing of his fate. I was sad to have missed the opportunity to reconnect, and—as is the case with so many people I attempted to make amends to— angry that I hadn't done it sooner.

So many people showed up just to illuminate, teach, or just care for a minute. Of course I don't always know it at the time, but everyone matters.

I try to keep that in mind.

INTERMISSION

Here are a few of the ways in which I sought to either avoid feelings or to capture and recreate other feelings.

CHEESE: My earliest kitchen memories include standing at my mothers knees in our Far Rockaway project dinette waiting for her to pass me the next thick slice of full fat Polly-O as she layered her Bronx-Jew version of lasagna.

CHOCOLATE: Takes the edge off. Puts the fog on. Sometimes convinced that it makes life worth living. Regret typically follows. First thing I stole was a Nestles Crunch bar. Last thing before typing this was Green and Black's dark.

COCA-COLA: Once a year. Dad always said the elusive seven ounce bottles were the best. I agree. Commonly dispensed warm when I was little to counteract stomach aches and nausea.

ICE CREAM: Some early childhood hole in my soul that acts like a bottomless wafer cone I continue to run to for seconds. Dolly Madison or Breyers occasionally occupied our childhood freezer by the paper half gallon, none of this $5.79 per pint bullshit. We ate out of big-ass *bowls*. Dad said that for my first birthday he sat me on a stool at

Baskin & Robbins where I downed my rations too quickly. Brain freeze followed, my eyes went white, I "moo'd" ("like a cow" he said) and passed out, dropping backward off the stool, my fall broken by his feet. (I would reenact this particular move some years later while sitting on a different stool in a different establishment.)

COFFEE/SANKA: Dad's powdered, low caffeine leftovers, cold with milk and sugar at the end of his cup. It was the perfect blend of bitter, sweet, fat and naughty (not very unlike my first screw) and I took immeasurable pleasure in bonding with my dad in this uniquely dad-ish thing, albeit in the form of his abandoned backwash. There were times during the five teen years I worked at Cracker Barrel Bakery when I drank up to ten cups per day. This contributed no doubt to ulcers and my chronic IBS, jumping off of city buses between stops to run into shops and offices looking for a bathroom, bowled over in a sweat for hours at a time. Love the stuff. Not good for me. I do drink a cup if I'm driving long distances late at night and occasionally when I can't move.

PIZZA: Quick and deliberate colon clogger and zit-fertilizer. Quick to sleep. Easy breakfast. Some have been as close to heaven as any bite can be. Gloria's on Main Street, Flushing was the worlds best *(I know, you know a better place ... whatever)*.

Rarely stop at one. Getting hungry.

FRENCH FRIES: I never eat one without realizing that it's not really food. So I eat two.

SUGARCANE: As a kid, a catholic neighbors' dad brought us canes or palms or whatever they're called on Palm Sunday or Cane Monday or whatever and we chewed the woody things and were immediately filled with way too much of the happy juice it yielded. I chewed until my eyes were going to pop and had one of my top five non-concussion headaches to date. Unlike other, more sophisticated substances I'd eventually discover, nausea and disorientation did actually deter me from ever consuming sugar in this particular form again.

BIRTH CONTROL PILLS: (stolen from my friends teenage sisters drawer): At thirteen, we took a few and began stumbling and laughing—placebo stupidity for ambitious self-destructors.

MAGIC MARKERS: Surpassing the pleasure elicited via my sense of smell, art sessions were enhanced as I felt their soothing effects in my throat, my chest, my shoulders—I inhaled the fumes slowly through my mouth and as deeply as my lungs could stretch, put the lid back on, breathed a few normal breaths, and repeated.

MODEL AIRPLANE GLUE: A warm blanket of ease that found me while trying to organize the little parts into the shiny thing shown on the outside of the box. I never finished a single model, but held the tube of glue open in my cupped palms over my mouth and nose and breathed long and deep, always making a deal with myself, setting a limit, but breaking it immediately to inhale just a moment more. It always resulted in a headache, foul breath and regret. *What were we talking about?*

SHOWER MASSAGE: I'd run its strong "needle" jet into my ear. There have been many times when I've scratched bug-bitten sections of skin, but letting the strong jet enter my ear was like scratching a long-suffered itch in my skull. Craning my neck like a purring cat, I could hear the roll of aqua-thunder and feel it *in* my sinuses and would be totally frozen there, head tilted to allow for just the right angle so that water could penetrate just so. I'd count to ten, determined to terminate the obviously dangerous act, switch ears and resume for a prescribed period, vow to be done, and then switch again. If you've ever scratched an itch during an orgasm then multiplied it by ten, you might understand how this felt. One of the more immediately self-destructive things I've done—beginning around age twelve—additionally insidious because no one ever would have to know and I'd be all alone with my shame, swollen eardrums, headache, the shame and brain damage looming. Don't do it.

ALCOHOL: My first drunk was at twelve with

Randy, we were outside on the hill throwing knives at trees and into the dirt. I remember the satisfaction and rush of achieving a good throw and got into a drill of backhanded throwing into the ground a foot or so in front of me. After one such throw, I bent in the growing dusk to retrieve my weapon and couldn't find it. I stepped back to get a better look and it was nowhere to be found. I let Randy in on my search and the two of us scanned the patchy lawn for a few minutes before he pointed at my foot. I followed the trail of his pointer and discovered the thing sticking straight up out of my blood-soaked Pro-Ked sneaker. Super powered, indestructible and delighted, an indelible note was made on my identity. I needed more of this in my life. I never drank to achieve just a buzz, always to get drunk. A tumultuous decade-long affair ensued. There's little about life that is worse than a hangover, but feeling good feels good.

VALIUM: I'd known about the many bottles of yellow pills my mother had in a bag in a box in the closet under her sewing scraps and replacement zippers and such, and I discovered their usefulness at around age fifteen when they appeared just in time to help me cope with another of dad's long hospitalizations; a barrage of teen agony and a cursed stretch of insomnia. I took a lot of these and they never seemed to run out.

The Trouble With Kim

SEX: Perhaps if someone besides porn and fantasy had told me what it's really for, what I'm really worth, and how it's really done, I would have had many more early connected, interesting and fun experiences. I couldn't wait for it because I thought it would make me whole, make me real. Talk about a blessing-turned-curse. When it finally happened (with a partner), it happened the wrong way. Failing to stop to consider adjusting motives, execution, or consequences, sex was a very over-pursued cycle of forgetting, wounding, and obsessing. Good change has transpired in this area.

MARIJUANA: Heavenly ether, my best friend second to music. But overuse and a complete forgetting of my path fucked that one up. I miss this the most, but enjoy having my lungs, my clear thoughts, my unaided creativity. Would if I thought I could, but not today.

CIGARETTES: I became a cigarette smoker when I stopped smoking everything else. Never ever had a drag without thinking, "This is killing me." Finally quit on the same day as my wife Jenn, around twenty years ago. It was surprisingly easy. Nearly smoked one on 9/11 as I thought that nothing really mattered.

I'm gonna stop detailing the slew of particular things I smoked, snorted, huffed, cooked and swallowed here because they all kinda blend into an amalgam of regretful behavior that is more about *me* and less about the stuff. I'm ok with the existence of recreational drugs. I know a lot of people benefit from them in incalculable ways. I know people who do just fine with theirs. I wish I could.

I've been fortunate to know many people who have gotten to the other side of their nightmares and to recognize their lives as the gifts that they are. They've gotten over all manner of habits with things some would consider "harmless" and others with things typically pegged as "hard." Because it's largely the person, not the stuff. I've also had more friends than I can count drive poison into veins, toxins into lungs, cars into trees, bullets into brains, and blades into wrists; each one might have had a more fortunate outcome had they gotten space between themselves and their substance. A few of my best friends and heroes didn't get that space. Neither did my brother, and it's that space that worries me. It's a space we avoid because the discomfort is unbearable. Because we're not ready to face that which it masks. Because life is, among other things, suffering. And how can we argue against dulling pain or enhancing the ordinary? I say do what you gotta do. And if your life is perfect, then do what you will to make it even better.

Sometimes I really fucking wish it were that way for me. I know so many people have wonderful experiences with the assistance of their favorite substances. I did when I started. Benefits stopped manifesting, replaced by negative consequences but I kept doing it anyway. Some people get high and lower their stress levels. I spend rent money. Some heighten their creativity, but I fall into dark, ugly places. Some generate responsible, productive and efficient routines. I lose jobs, sleep with other men's wives and set cars on fire.

More power to us all, because regardless of our survival strategies, we're made of the same diseased, imperfect, ridiculous, miraculous stuff.

A great irony here is that even without being drunk, stoned or otherwise impaired, I still find ways to escape, to lose touch and to self-destruct. My considerable and long held disdain for my limits has transformed—mostly—to respect. Perhaps I could have it another way after all this space between my last time and me.

But I don't actually care to know, because *maybe not.*

CLEAN, 1987 - AGE TWENTY-TWO

THE LAST TIME I got high was June 3,1987. It, as the thousand times before, was a doozy. I'd come close to ending it all and had spent years systematically destroying my body, my spirit and my potential. After a few weeks clean I sought to grab hold of a routine I hoped could carry me safely until such time that my urges and obsessions might subside—something I didn't really believe would actually happen, but wanted desperately.

I bought a little brown phone book and began to collect the names and numbers of new, safe friends. I was terrified of people and felt ridiculous asking for help, but did every single thing that I thought could help. I was desperate for relief. I carried the little brown phone book in my back pocket and it came to represent my connection to what was possible. I jotted down some distinguishing features that would help me to connect the names in my book to faces, as my retention for such complex details was severely compromised.

"Frank: redhead, bass"

"Rob: super tall"

"Marc: Fired NYPD. Scary. Pretty wife"

"Tommy. Shades. Guitar?"

"Jon: Crackhead. Black. Franklin Square."

"Steve: Needy. Mustache."

"Danny: Green eyes. Friend?"

The Trouble With Kim

These and many others ambitiously filled my little brown book. Dialing some of these numbers helped me to limit the danger of setting foot back on the path to doom. We all wanted the same things from one another—to help learn how to live without our poison, to stop hurting, and to foster hope where hopelessness had long been the default condition.

Quickly, the lines on the pages of my little brown book filled.

After just a few months, most of these people were gone. Some I couldn't recall meeting. Some had gone back to a life of active addiction and so all I could do was join the collective worry and hope to see them again. A few had cleaned up and that had been enough for them. Now they were—possibly—all better.

But by the time I had a year clean in 1988, I sat with my improving memory and my little brown phone book and a pen and listed over thirty people with whom I'd shared intimately, who I was aware in a short span of time, had died. DWI's. Homicides. Suicides. Accidental ODs. AIDS.

I felt cursed and newly crushed every time another friend perished. Sad for me. Enraged at addiction. Afraid of the next time. I eventually rationalized that I have many people in my life, so I have more to lose, that this was the necessarily corrosive by-product of an expansive community.

People are remembered for their considerable accomplishments, victories and fortunes. But if you're an addict, THATs what we remember most. And it works differently depending on your lot. Idols and legends can get away a with it—romanticize it even—Kerouacs, Holidays and Cobains whose work will stand up taller than their mistakes will for ages, and are even more interesting— perhaps more beloved—BECAUSE OF their tortured existence and how they met their end.

But then there's my brother and pages of other sisters and brothers whose purpose and good work was preempted by the enormous pull of their compulsions and the commitment it took to feed them; all people remember is how they were fuck-ups.

I think there's truth to the belief that our stories help others to know that they're not alone and that they, too can fix their broken lives. I thought there was no one in the world like me until I heard someone explain my precise despair in theirs. Today I'm rather convinced that I've done a good deal of it wrong (my mind, unattended, still appears to be out to get me) but some hard, fundamental changes have helped me to avoid making that one big mistake for my most recent twelve thousand some odd days.

Therapy: An Unillustrated History, 1987

I WAS A twenty-two year old from Queens having an affair with a beautiful, married thirty-three year old woman from Poland. She had straight, brown hair that stopped at the very top of her short skirts. Wherever she went, heads turned and eyes locked on her pretty face and her long, dancer's legs. She had a white corvette, a lovely, cheerful, nine-year-old daughter and a short, plump husband who was far nicer than I was.

I'd crossed these lines on several occasions knowing it was going to harm them and me. I tried to talk myself out of it. I really did. But I made mistakes. These encounters all held certain thrilling weight, in some ways akin to my pursuit of drugs and while I knew they were fundamentally wrong, I did little to avoid them (like I had with drugs). This affair force-fed my ego while simultaneously charring my conscience. Marta told me I was funny, and looked at me longer than most people did. She radiated sexuality and told me she was unhappy in her marriage. I wish I had done it differently.

We met in an office in West Hempstead during my tumultuous stint as a real estate agent. We had a rapport, and she suggested that we attempt to secure listings together, as a team. Strategies such as this were commonly appealing to sellers, and so we went on a few appointments together. I couldn't look an adult in the eye for more than a second

161

or two, so just smiled a lot and let Marta do the talking. Her charming accent and bubbly energy were impossible to resist, we were a likable team, but secured no listings.

One day she said she wanted to show me a special house. I'd been barely surviving for years now, and the relief I was beginning to feel, without the constant craziness of active addiction, rendered me a little confused. Rent was late, but earning money was a lower priority than driving around with a pretty lady, so I went anywhere Marta asked me to go. We used the realtor's lock-box key and entered a compact, brick house with signs indicating that it was for sale and had been a medical office. The waiting room still had piles of magazines and a wall rack with pamphlets. I looked through the Lucite separating that room from the receptionist's desk full of papers, a phone, and a stapler, and was saddened by the apparent immediacy of the doctor's career-ending mystery.

Marta stood at an open doorway and beckoned me with one finger, stepping backward into the room. My mind filled with lust, but I was sure I was misreading the situation. We stood in a crude examination room that hadn't been painted in decades. The table had smoothly worn stirrups and rips in the vinyl upholstery; the yellowed venetian blinds were tattered, letting light through in chopped up bits.

Marta walked up to a shelving unit that housed stainless steel medical instruments, and held up what looked like an implement of torture, but which I surmised was gynecological in nature, though I couldn't really say exactly what it was for. She swung it in my face and laughed as I bent back. She did it again and again, until I grabbed her arm and she twirled until her back was against my front, and then stopped giggling, turned her face toward mine, looked into my eyes and kissed me.

I was willing to burn in hell in order to experience that moment, to swig her beauty, to know that I mattered to her. I hated myself for being with this married woman, and my rationalization that it was she who chose me—she who planned this, she who made the move—didn't quiet the pain of knowing that she had a husband who loved her. He was there in that examination room. He was in my basement apartment watching us sweat. He was standing outside of her white corvette, peering in through the fogged windows. He stood behind her, crying as we talked about art, laughed until we cried and said that we loved one another.

Despite talking it through and arriving at the same sensible conclusion again and again, we continued for half of the summer before I quit the job. I wasn't built for the type of work required to convince grownups to trust me, and I needed to get away from Marta before more harm was done. She wasn't going to stop. I had to be the adult, or at least that's what I told myself. I never saw or heard from her again, though I wish I had.

When I went to a clinic to find my first therapist as an adult, the guy doing the intake was named Cal and he asked if there was a particular type of person I related to better than another, someone I can feel safe with. I thought that was a sensible question and, after a moment said, "Anyone except for an attractive female." He stared at me for a long time. He looked down, scribbled something and said, "*okay.*"

The following Thursday afternoon I met with Barbara, a perfectly attractive woman, but someone to whom I wasn't at all attracted. I will forever have a guilty and odd kinship with Cal for honoring my truth. Barbara was one of a handful of people I looked to in hopes of changing my mind, and therefore my behavior, and therefore my life. Although that's a tall order and a big responsibility, she did her best. I did not.

Another was Celia. She was stationed in her house in a wealthy and hilly North Shore town near where I'd been living with my girlfriend, Jackie.

Jackie drove a Maserati (I'd never before seen one) and a Porsche and maybe it was our polar opposite upbringing that brought us together and bound us in a story union. We were both in early recovery and enjoyed some sweet moments, but then we fought, we hated, we grew lonely, we made up, we cried, we tried again, we loved, we fought, we hated, and so it went. We grew more and more delicate with each session. When Jackie and I eventually saw Celia a few times for couples therapy, she sided clearly with Jackie and by the end of the second session we were broken up.

That night we left in our separate cars; it was snowing gently and all was still. I began my short, lonely ride to what would only be my home for a little while longer. There was a car stopped on the side of the road, and a woman kneeling before it. I got out and joined her on the ground with a dead fox, stellar and warm with a steady stream of blood flowing from one nostril. My world was positioning to fall apart again as I bore witness to tragedy and somehow I felt the comforting hand of my process on my heart, just as mine stroked the chest of this angel. The woman and I cried together in silence and said nothing.

I elected to attend a men's group Celia ran and at one point she announced the change in the pronunciation of her name from *"SEEL-ee-ah"* (accent on the first syllable) to *"cel-EYE-ya"* (accent on the second, newly pronounced syllable) and would correct you if you forgot. She defended her new name as if the old one bore controversy or something yucky and heavy. No one even asked.

She was a woman in the midst of some sort of inner turbulence and she wasn't fucking around. She called me at home one day to say that a check I'd written had bounced. Familiar but not pleasant news for me, I apologized and asked her to redeposit it, that I'd put money in the account that very day and it was now going to clear. She interrupted and firmly ordered me to come right away with cash. I felt bad and small and never trusted her again. The feeling was mutual.

Years later, through the hospice network that cared for Mom during her last days, I met with a grieving-counselor named Arturo. He was enormous in body (and in kindness) and during my months of meeting with him, I finally got it that sometimes sharing is simply sharing. That while magic can happen, it usually doesn't. And that what I needed to do was to talk about things, rather than just sit with, or repair them. That although I'm quiet and calm on the outside, there could be a monsoon of turmoil brewing inside, tormenting me, confusing me, and doing damage to my spirit and to my body. For the first time, I showed up just to talk. I had friends to talk to, but anyone close to me had been burdened by the unfolding of these events themselves and had their own issues with it and with how I'd handled it. With Arturo I could say anything, and I didn't worry about bumming him out or about being judged.

Once married for a decade or so, I began seeing a therapist named Scott after an extended period of insomnia, nightmares, depression and sexually challenging body stuff. I just couldn't do it. My marriage had suffered enough, and shame and desperation brought me to seek help again. Upon meeting for the first time he asked the types of questions such professionals need answers to. He listened intently, unaffected by the briefing, which covered a childhood adorned with psychiatric hospitals, looming abandonment, OCD, poverty and self-mutilation. He maintained his poker face as I summarized my drug abuse, my family's psycho-enmeshment, cancer after cancer, and the recent death of my entire family of origin.

Our eyes locked for a long time during which I was prepared for him to offer a referral to someone who he'd heard had performed miracles and he'd see if he could get me in.

I told him that I was turned off by people who find

themselves in a cycle of therapeutic dependency and that I only wanted to work on this stuff for a while with a termination date not so far out. That was when he smiled and told me that he hoped I wouldn't take it wrong but that in his professional opinion I was an "excellent candidate for ongoing therapy."

I didn't take it wrong but I didn't like it. We worked together for a while without any earth shaking achievements, but it certainly didn't hurt. Jenn soon became pregnant with our first son and I ended my time with Scott.

There have been other therapists since, and I'm currently working with a guy who is powerfully sensitive, intuitive and skilled. I don't lose sleep wondering whether this needs to continue forever, as I'm neither deluded by notions of infinite suffering nor ultimate healing. This is a dynamic and multifaceted deal. My regrets and my worries are nothing to be afraid of. They are a part of my past. They are a part of my present, but only a part. I don't expect they will be totally alleviated going forward.

But in the company of my new mind—the one that knows that life is a package deal and that no matter what befalls me, I'm essentially good and I deserve to be ok—they have little more than the power to sting me. And if I drop my guard and find myself paralyzed one again, I'll be ok. I have help.

GROUP, 1988 - AGE TWENTY-THREE

DURING MY FIRST year clean I heard constant references to "Judy group" or to members of the North Shore gang of eager self-improvers I'd begun to hang with at, and after, meetings benefiting from "Judy work." It was not long before I developed a sense that some of these messed-up, but trying, people were a little too willing to turn their life and their will over to this Judy person, a renowned psychotherapist who, aside from her popular work with addiction in her private practice, was running therapeutic encounter groups. They leaned heavily on the remedy that would be dispensed each Tuesday night at the church in Manhasset by the Great One, whom they called "Judy."

At first I was hardly eager to take on yet another paradigm-shifting measure—giving up my sweetheart (drugs) was one thing. For a number of reasons, I grew skeptical, offended even, by the mere mention of her name. Judy-ism was surely not for me.

But I was eventually intrigued. These people seemed to share a common calm. And they knew each other. They were a set of peers more closely knit that the rest of us run-of-the-mill, everyday recovery people. And they smiled. I asked Danny—whom I respected more than anyone I'd ever known—if he thought I should come to a Judy group. He was my first sponsor, one of my best friends and had the kindest eyes of anyone I'd ever met. He said that since I was in very early recovery I should just enjoy it, that "group" tends to stir up very deep-set and often painful issues that someone in early recovery might not be prepared to deal with. The feelings that could arise from the types of probing discussions that tend to transpire at group might jeopardize my progress.

Attacking my new life with a fervor on par with my addiction, I intended to get every ounce of "better" so I soon said I was ready, and Danny agreed that we'd go together. We drove to the church and did some parking lot hugging and hellos. I knew a few of the attendees and had seen the rest in passing. Being there with Danny, I was introduced to every one of the twenty or so recovering people. We entered the vast room that I imagined would host large events like blood drives, bake sales and bingo. We took our seats in the wide circle of folding chairs in the middle of the great room.

Judy couldn't have been more than five feet tall and had a rounded back and a dirty blonde Dorothy Hamill haircut. She peered through thick-framed glasses with her squinting eyes and was much younger than I'd expected her to be, thirty-five at most. She had a strikingly compassionate smile and spoke her few words with intense thoughtfulness. I couldn't help but recognize just how awesome she was. Careful. Insightful. Smart. Extremely loving. I got it.

Several in the circle recalled something they'd heard—or committed to—the previous week, and after a few minutes, Judy asked us to find a partner and I did. I watched myself being cocky and judgmental and I thought I had it in the bag; I was on my way to a whole new me.

Seth Branitz

We were to sit facing one another and then to close our eyes and recall a time from our childhood when we were perfectly happy, excited, and free, and safe. She said that it could deal with anything at all, a party, a grandparent, an animal, ice cream, whatever. Then we were to open our eyes and tell our partner about it in detail. Judy would then give us further instructions. The room was quiet and the only thing louder than an occasional giggle from someone's clear recollection was the screaming of my own mind, as I scoured the cabinets of my early past for a happy memory.

I had none.

Judy gently commanded that we open our eyes and begin to share. I looked at my partner through teary eyes. He asked if I was all right and I nodded *no* and the rest of the night has faded to a series of shoulders and bosoms, into which I wept years of an empty childhood. I was so sad for the little boy I'd recalled, for his constant worry and the never-ending fear of something going very wrong. Of not being able to articulate what hurt. Of being bullied, or neighbors calling the cops to report the violent fights in our home. Of Dad never coming back after one of his extended hospitalizations. Of pushing fragile Mom over the edge, and into one of her own rages or rants, and then into her bed where she'd remain for the rest of the day and night, sniffling and chewing pack after pack of Double-Mint gum, or sleeping on and on. Of being the reason my brother was away and only got to come back on a weekend here and there. My fault. I couldn't find a simple joy. A pure laugh. A safe moment. A single rainbow.

I didn't go back to Judy. Danny was right, and I was humbled into the willingness to pace myself. Dealing with simply *not using* and beginning the long, never ending process of healing, was quite enough for now.

I feel like I never properly graduated from childhood to now-hood. Like there's an organic sequence of discoveries, realizations, and rites that move one from innocence to fulfillment, with bumps and bruises along the way, no doubt. But I must have blinked or else I skipped that class. And here I am, still a child doing grownup things, and needing to unpack the luggage that my soul and I have dragged around for all this time.

Or to burn it. And if I do talk about it, I need to put a greater effort into being here now so at least I miss nothing on my reluctantly growing list of happy moments.

Fewer regrets. More animals. Less shame. More ice cream.

DEE DEE, 1989 - AGE TWENTY-FOUR

THE RAMONES HAD been one of my favorite bands since Suzanne Vilchez had introduced them to me in seventh grade. Suzanne had a Ramones button on her denim jacket and the "VH," Van Halen symbol painted on her denim loose-leaf notebook. I'd inquired about them both, and the combination of her enthusiasm and how adorable she was, sold me on what would be a life-changing discovery. I'm sure it was a good time for me to find this music, but admit that I might have become a fan of any band Suzanne liked—or any cult, for that matter. She had hell-raiser eyes, a contagious laugh, and was very popular.

When junior high ended she was at a party, and a few guys playfully scooped her up and threw her into a pool, where she hit the bottom hard, broke, and floated to the top, never to walk again. I took this very personally, and it still hurts to recall getting the news and later visiting her in the hospital, where Jay and I learned the word "paraplegic." She's never stopped doing incredible things and I adore her, the girl who gave me Van Halen and the frickin' Ramones (not to mention some middle- school daydreams).

I snuck into a showing of the campy Ramones' film, *Rock and Roll High School* at the Queens College Student Union building and by the end of the screening I had a horny girl named Ilana sitting on my lap (I could work with this) and a plan to pierce my ear and line my life with safety pins.

I began playing muted, eighth note power chords on my nylon string classical acoustic guitar and bought *Rocket to Russia* and *End of the Century.* I took to the Ramones' quick, raucous tunes, and listened like I was examining some ancient map. I felt a heart-racing connection to the simple rounds that flowed with an almost tribal sensibility. I put them right along side of my Beatles, and my John Denver, and got a Japanese Strat and a Gorilla amp that produced an adequately satisfying distortion.

Then in 1988 I was at a friend's place in Jamaica, Queens. I was twenty-four, and recently clean. Not long, but long enough to recognize a hunger to make up for all the time I'd lost ignoring the call of my heart and the reckoning of my spirit. I was collecting courage to just leave without challenge when I spotted this badass punk dude who looked a lot like Dee Dee Ramone (promptly dismissed because I realize that I always think people look like other people). He was climbing the walls, by himself, and bopping up and down to some drummer in his head. He walked past me and stopped, said a straight-faced "'Sup," then looked anxiously around the room when I returned a nod and involuntarily looked down. That's when I noticed a large gaudy ring on his finger, diamonds spelling out "DeeDee."

He extended his hand and said, "Dee Dee" and I said, "I know who you are, Dee Dee." I shook his hand and said my name. He asked if I was a musician. At the time I much more looked than played the part. I said I was, and we talked about what I was working on, and about his new rap project, "Dee Dee King." He asked if I had a tape (That's what we used to call demos) and then he asked if I was hungry.

I was able to temper my star-struck smallness and recognize that this was a dude, and he needed someone to talk to. I went back and forth between the two many times, but was ultimately glad to be connecting with another passionate, strange artist who was trying to stay clean. The fact that he was a world famous, millionaire punk hero was novel.

We went to the Hilltop Diner and ate French Fries with gravy, and talked for a couple of hours. We exchanged numbers and met at the Hilltop a bunch more times when he was in town, and each time he asked if I had a tape. I'd just begun to mess around with a Tascam Porta One four-track cassette recorder which I had been intimidated by for years, and while he was sincere and interested, and a viable source of real support, I did not produce a tape.

The Ramones' band manifesto included the rule, "no smiling," so getting to hang out and see him be fairly normal was cool. Not only did he smile, but he laughed goofily, especially at his own jokes. We talked about why we used drugs, why there can't be a god, about our parents, our shared admiration for Ally Sheedy, and about music. I slipped back and forth between easy intimacy and a sort of "I'm not worthy," out-of-body experience.

Once when I spoke with his wife, Vera, on the phone, she thanked me for hanging out with him. She said he needed good, clean guys to spend time with. She got me into two Ramones shows free—all I asked for—and was normal and lovely with a strong Queens accent. They lived in a condo in Whitestone and it couldn't have been easy to be married to Dee Dee. With me he was kind and levelheaded. With others he was abrupt, opinionated and pretty burnt out.

Touring took him over, he went back to heroin, and we lost touch.

In autumn 1999, I was rehearsing with a five-piece band called Sol-Tree in a vacant storefront on Avenue B and 10th Street in Manhattan, and we came outside for a fresh-air break.

I heard someone call my name, turned and saw Dee-Dee crossing the street. He was platinum blonde and yelled "*SETH DAVIS!!! Whatcha doin, coppin dope?*" I smiled and said no and didn't bother saying that I was still clean, as he clearly wasn't. He introduced me to his girlfriend, and then swiftly pulled her to his side. The whiplashed beauty cracked gum and smiled sweetly. He said he was retired and living in Holland now.

I said that I was playing later that night and invited him, joking that I'd get him past security. He laughed maniacally, then stopped on a dime and asked if I had a tape. Finally able to say yes, I asked him to hold on and raced into the space, rummaged through my bag, secured a copy of a demo tape I'd been shopping and selling at shows, and went back outside. He was gone.

Seth Branitz

I was sad, but not surprised by his fatal overdose, just months after my own brother's. He'd been a rock star for most of his life and I hear that that comes with baggage. He exemplified and defined facets of the rock and roll lifestyle and he was rather pessimistic. I saw him behave like a royal jerk when accepting the Ramones induction into the Rock and Roll Hall of Fame on TV and I wanted to hide my face. I'm sure he more than earned his reputation.

It's difficult to quantify just how much of an impact a person has on you. Some heavy talks and some laughs are imprinted on my soul, and I know we served a purpose for one another during a challenging and critical mile on our respective paths. I don't know if I'd love that music any less if we hadn't been friends. I connect with so many artists, whose gift is far more profound than their acquaintance might be—and above our bond, high above the novelty of having had a hero for a friend, and aside from any of the cool moments we had together—I get chills when I hear recordings of Dee Dee counting off Ramones songs (one, two, three, four!). I get a chill and remember that there's work to do and that being alive is just the start. It's like he's counting off my life, calling out my passion, counting in Sue's pulse, making my heart race, and waking me up, over and over again.

Tommy Guitar, 1988 - age twenty-three

Since the age of twelve I was clear on the way I could create, share; to connect and to make my contribution to mankind. By the time I was a teenager, I was painfully shy, hopelessly distracted by my drug use, lazy, and not too interested in practicing, only in writing songs.

I tried being in a few bands and it was rough, a lot of work, and so far as I could ascertain, no reward. Bandmates inevitably become cranky and so did I, so I stuck to what was fluid and uncomplicated, which for me was songwriting.

A local rock band, which had sweet four-part harmonies, played a few of my songs, and I played in acoustic duos, a seven-piece classic rock outfit, and a loud, sloppy, three-piece garage band. While we were playing, all that mattered were good songs, it seemed, but I wasn't good at asking for what I needed. It was clear, judging by the immense talent of the company I was keeping, that I just wasn't a very good musician.

Mostly, I just wrote and filled notebooks. Once I realized I could harmonize fairly well, I set up two tape recorders, played and sang into one, then played that one back while singing a harmony and recording that into the other one. Then I'd do it again and again until I had a choir of me sounding like we were singing on the wing of the space shuttle, with no concern for ambient noise, radiators hissing, people talking in the next room, or mistakes. It was my way, sloppy though it was, to make manifest that which played ceaselessly in my head.

I drove to a music store in Mahwah, in New Jersey and I purchased a Tascam Porta One four-track cassette recorder. This enabled me to make these multi track recordings but with less background noise and more tracks.

Then I could make tapes of the resulting mixes and let other people hear them. Intimidated even by the low-level technology of the thing, I didn't touch it for a long while, until I'd been clean for a few months. Once I began to get my health back and my head began to clear, I was anxious to make up for all the time I'd wasted being unproductive. My days and nights had been spent obsessing on all I was NOT doing —at present they still are—and I wanted to make art more than I wanted anything.

I had seen Tommy at meetings and was drawn to his aesthetic—long, unkempt hair, dark glasses—a rock star. One day, after admiring him from afar for a while, he walked up to me and we introduced ourselves. He said, "you're a musician, right?" I was tickled that he knew this, and he said that we should get together and play sometime. We exchanged numbers and I made the first move, calling him to say, "I have these songs and I don't know what to do with them."

We got together at the apartment he shared with his wife Sheri, their turtles, and tons of music gear. I played him my songs and he listened approvingly, saying, "Got any others?" a handful of times. His phone rang and he spoke for a while saying he'd get back to the person on the other end later. He then told me that that was Lance (an odd but brilliant crooner known locally as Lance Romance) who had called proposing that they start a band. I thought that was cool and asked him if he knew other people to play with them. He counted on his fingers, "Well there's me, Lance, Francis, me and you ... that sounds like a band to me."

Lance didn't end up in the band, but all of the others that came and went were older and far more experienced than I. We were all in recovery, which made for a motley crew with torrid pasts and personal and practical issues ranging from probation and mental and physical disease to extreme sensitivity, exhibitionism and—most devastating—relapses.

Nevertheless, we found our sounds and played some parties and a few clubs, including a strip bar in Massapequa named Diamond Lil's which on Saturday nights became an alcohol-and-drug-free spot called The Dry Rock Cafe. It was dirty and packed with a crowd who were happy to be doing something with their nights other than their meetings, the diner, and resisting the temptations that were so much stronger toward the end of the day. Although on these nights none was served, it stunk of beer, which many of us found comforting.

We rehearsed in the basement of a big house I shared with a bunch of other addicts in Glen Cove. Even though it was my place, and most of the originals we were playing were mine, I always felt like a guest, like a kid. I was fortunate to be in their company, and did my best to trust them.

Seth Branitz

Tommy and I sang, as did Frances, an exotic dancer with Haight-Ashbury style and a killer voice. I was very fond of her but hated the idea of her being in the band. I thought that the band, having several singers, especially one as showy as her, detracted from whatever legitimate edge we offered. She was dynamic, immensely talented and very nice, but I fought for patience as I waited for her songs to be done so that I could enjoy playing one of Tommy's or mine. She was classically great, with fucking amazing range, but I questioned her emotional depth. She belonged in Vegas or on TV, not in a little druggy garage band on Long Island. Watching her made me uncomfortable, as she brought to our shows and rehearsals some of the same shimmies and gyrations that she used when topless. She stood; wide-legged, swaying right against me, peering into my eyes as I played. I wanted to disappear. Only now can I look back and realize that it might have looked cool. At the time, it made me mildly nauseous. She once told me in passing that she was in love with me, which repelled me even more. Although I cared very much for her, it was more of a sisterly, protective love and admiration.

There was a guy who Frances called "a friend" who was a financial mentor and advising her on how to manage the good money she was making as a dancer. He was older than she and frequented the club where she danced. As lines sometimes get blurry in matter of loneliness, need, and money, these two were curiously enmeshed in discussions that landed Frances a down payment on a very nice raised ranch in Massapequa. She avoided all talk of her benefactor and never brought him to shows.

Tommy and I began to record our songs at the studio of an old friend of his in Ronkonkoma on any Sunday morning that we could scrape enough money together. Although I remember the grey skies on these drives, I also look back on these mornings at Paris Studios as the most exciting times I'd had. I was gaining distance from my compulsion to escape with substances, and I was immersed in a beautiful collaboration, finally doing what I'd envisioned myself doing since I began writing songs. I was doing it with someone who I had the utmost admiration for, personally and creatively. Tommy was brilliant, badass and cool, and we were partners.

Another hardened addict named Gary played some electric guitar and keyboard with us, and one day after a spirited and fun rehearsal, Tommy got sentimental and thanked Gary. He told him that he was exactly what he needed in his life. I was standing right there and stunned. Tommy then turned to me and said, "You too," but whatever vulnerability he may have been genuinely showing was lost on timing. My gratitude for Tommy's mentorship and musical example persists, but the personal bond I craved with him never came to fruition. If I brought up my issues outside of the band, he listened quietly but with only partial presence. If I asked how he was or about his illness, he paused a long while before responding that he was dealing with it or changing the subject. He got progressively weaker, left his day job on disability and resumed a routine of heroin, methadone, and isolation.

Seth Branitz

He'd gotten us a gig opening up for a national band he loved at Sundance, a rock club on the south shore. We all arrived early, except for Tommy. We set up and as show time approached, stalled the promoter, saying that he was on his way. We couldn't do the gig without him and when dirty looks turned to hovering, we loathsomely submitted and began a quick breakdown. The other bands' roadies, the audience and the service staff all seemed angry with us. With two hands full of gear I headed for my car, kicked open the double side doors, and there stood Tommy in the light of the lamppost, guitar case in one hand, amp in the other, cab pulling away, aviators hiding his eyes. When he saw that he'd arrived too late, he bent his knees, put down his stuff, and froze. Frances hugged his rigid body and he remained frozen as she softly reassured him. They put his stuff in her car, and they left. She told me that he sobbed, saying that he'd blown what he reckoned was some kind of golden opportunity, that he had ruined everything, that he was done.

At the next rehearsal, Tommy and I talked about the recordings and he told me that I'd likely have to finish them without him. I felt that this was an overreaction and couldn't imagine doing much of anything without him. This was the only time that I felt he opened up to me. He said, "I'm not getting better. It's just a matter of time."

Just weeks later, it was Gary who called me with the news that Tommy had died. The word was that he'd gotten some sort of stomach bug that he was too weak to fight. His widow Sheri—a dear friend ever since—recently told me that she didn't press for information after he died in the hospital. It may have been a complication from AIDS or a heroin overdose. No sense pressing for truth that won't heal anything at this point.

I was so thoroughly devastated and don't think I've ever quite recovered. When I finally forced myself out of bed to attend his funeral, I sat in the car crying, and made it inside just in time for the end. I'd missed my band mates holding hands at his coffin while one of our songs blasted through a Panasonic boom box speckled with paint from Tommy's former side job.

I indulged in a long, dark mourning. I'd been living with Jackie, and I remember the day a couple of months later when I smiled at her and made a joke. She asked, "Are you back?" and we cried.

I eventually saw that the distance Tommy had kept from me may not have been so much a function of me being an unworthy friend as his effort to protect me, knowing his days were numbered, and just having too much going on.

By then I'd begun playing solo gigs at cafes and bars, sometimes partnering with Lance Romance, who I stayed friends with until he died of lung disease.

Frances died of a heroin overdose while I was traveling in '95 and I didn't find out until I returned, months later.

It feels unfair to be stripped of the chance to say thank you, to say goodbye.

Early on in my anemic performance career, I began a routine of retreating to the bathroom or somewhere private before heading to the microphone, getting on my knees, and praying, not to god, but as a thank you to Tommy and Frances. Over the years the ritual has grown to include Lance, my brother Kim—my most considerable musical influencer—and others. I just say some version of, *"Thank you for giving me courage and permission to make my art. I hope I get to light someone up—to help someone to relate and to feel. I'm so grateful to you. I wouldn't be here without you. I'm going to play now. I hope you like it."*

Then I imagine that they're smiling.

JONATHAN, 1988 - AGE TWENTY-THREE

JONATHAN WAS A crackhead from Cincinnati and for a while there in the late 80s, we were like two peas in a pod.

Without our respective poisons there were now thoughts to think and questions to ask. We shared deep hurts and profound regrets and held one another to higher standards. We drove to meetings together and would then sit at a pizza place for hours or go for long walks up and down the working class streets of the mid-island towns where we both lived. We exchanged my wounded and searching songs for stories of his heart-crushing loneliness as a gay black addict in a straight white world.

We were brothers and I loved John. He was hysterical and clever and his toxic tirades were tinged with his family's gorgeous southern *'blackisms'* like, "Shut yo' mouth," and left field cries to *Sweet Baby Jesus.*

John disappeared for days at a time, not answering calls, not answering his door, upon which I'd bang hopefully for a half hour or more. I'd call obsessively and drive by several times a day hoping for his reappearance. I'd worry and eventually find him crashed lying unconscious in his car or struggling to his door, dirty, ashamed and exhausted. I'd help him formulate the lies he told his employer, took him back to meetings, got him food and hoped he wouldn't do it again.

Then once, he disappeared for more than a week. I was

desperate to find him, fearing for his life, unsure what to do with my feelings or my evenings. As I'd done before when another crack-head friend had gone missing, I drove to a block on the Elmont/Queens Village line known for drug activity, and I surveyed a few of the guys who were lurking in doorways, hoping for the attention of a legitimate customer as opposed to a cop. There was a guy who I'd seen before, early 20s like me—in a red hoodie, like me—and our respective nods called him to approach my car. He asked for my order, and I said, "Where's Jonathan?"

"Who?"

"Don't fuck with me. You know who I mean. Where – *the fuck* – is Jonathan?"

He began to respond and I swung open the car door, which hit him in the legs, got out and walked quickly toward him. "Yo, yo, yo!" he uttered, at first in a hush but ending in a shriek, and I backed him into a storefront gate. I pressed my chest and my face against his and said, "Where the fuck is Jonathan? Where *is* he? *Where is he?*"— my rage dissolving into whimpers and my body collapsing against his. He said something about me being fucking crazy, and hurried me by the hand back to my car saying, "I ain't know your boy, I ain't know nothin' bout your boy, go on." All the way home I shook and cried the way I had at other times I'd broken.

A few days later, when Jon finally called me from rehab, he'd blown all his money on drugs and sold his TV, his jewelry, and his car to get more. Now he was eight days into a month long stay. His therapist wanted his family there for a session but he had no family to speak of—his mom and her boyfriend had perished in a suicide pact and his sisters had had it with him—so they asked me to sit in.

Jonathan's usually GQ perfect hair and pencil-thin mustache were overgrown and his skin was covered with little scabs he couldn't stop touching. He was slouching and looked exhausted, eyes red and mouth agape. This last run had taken a toll.

His therapist was a pretty, young, soft-spoken woman with concern in her eyes and a pen and pad in hand. After a few minutes recapping this last run and how badly he felt about it, he told me that he didn't want to keep anything from me. I reminded him that he could tell me anything and with some soft encouragement from the professional in the room, Jonathan said that he had different kinds of feelings for me.

"I love you," he said.

I said, "I know. I love you too, Jon."

"No," he insisted. "I'm IN LOVE with you."

After my stunned silence he reiterated and said he needed to know if I loved him too.

I didn't.

I felt terrible. He cited an impressive list of things I had said that he'd interpreted to be hints and open doors. He thought compliments I'd made on his appearance were flirtatious. He was sure that long hugs we'd shared were longer than the kinds that a friend might give another. And he thought that me airing my girl troubles was an indication that I was shifting my attentions away from them altogether. He rifled off one incident, one remark after another. I assured him of their other, true and intended meanings.

He dropped his head onto his knees and cried, his arms dangling, body jumping as he drew in air.

I told him I would do anything to help him but that in this regard, he was mistaken.

It was awful, but with the skillful guidance of his young therapist, each of us said that we wanted to continue being friends. When the time came to wrap up the wily and failed intervention, the therapist asked if there was anything else Jonathan or I wanted to say to one another.

I stumbled in reply, "Yeah, I don't want to be a dick about this but you're my friend, and you've been seeing me in this *other* way for a while and so going forward how can I be sure that while I'm just being me, you're not, like, loving me or desiring me?"

Jon cut me off and yelled, "Oh don't be so fucking full of yourself!"

A month after rehab, cops found Jon unconscious and naked in a stairwell in Hempstead. He went around and around with detox, rehab, and meetings and I moved in with Jackie on the north shore. We drifted apart, Jon and I.

I can't find him. I've googled him, emailed and called the personnel departments at large companies where he was employed, and typed his name into the search bar of every social media platform, all in vain. I try every couple of years and he's nowhere.

The Trouble With Kim

He was too scared to get an AIDS test. I said I'd go with him. He said he couldn't bear to know. I don't know if he got sick or maybe wrote his own version of his mother's fate, but It's confounding to me how two people can be so exceedingly intimate—can play such remarkable roles in one another's dramas—yet wake up one day a million miles apart.

I mean my own life bears NO resemblance to the one I was running from back when Jonathan and I were buddies, but for a while there at the end of the 80s, we were like two peas in a pod.

JENN, 1991 - AGE-TWENTY SIX

AFTER LEAVING JACKIE I moved to the opposite side of Long Island and shared a house in Long Beach near where I worked. It was right on the main drag, across the street from the Italian place where I ordered baked ziti several nights a week and the supermarket where I'd stock up on cigarettes and pints of Häagen-Dazs.

I lived downstairs and had my own entrance, and the artist I sublet from was upstairs where the kitchen and living room were. It was sunny and furnished with tasteful antiques and his huge, cut-paper works of art. The first time I decided to cook there, I opened up the kitchen drawer to find roaches crawling about. I closed the drawer, took my ingredients, and henceforth only ever ventured upstairs to pay my rent.

I hated my job as a telemarketer, hawking overpriced collectible coins to nerds around the country, but had made a good friend in Mitch, who made me laugh and helped me through the breakup. Mitch brought me chocolate horns and other pastries from the bakery, and left silly messages on my home answering machine in order to give me breaks from my sulking.

He and his girlfriend, Kitten, set me up on my only blind date ever. It was Kitten's childhood friend, Lisa, a topless dancer with month old implants and a very pretty face. We sat at the vegetarian restaurant, ate blueberry pancakes and chugged black coffee as the three of them made small talk and I watched the clock over the counter. I agreed to go to a party with them later that day just to be nice, but bailed out and never saw Lisa again.

The first time I saw Jenn she was sitting next to the office manager, being trained to share the growing workload. She wore her dad's blue sport jacket, sleeves rolled up, over a white tee shirt. She had long, soft brown hair and the most beautiful face I'd ever seen. We shook hands and I melted. I loved her.

We sometimes spoke at work and she offered me sound reflections on my troubles with Jackie, the breakup, and some clumsy dating I did afterward. She was comfortable in her skin and made me happy. We became good friends. I told Mitch that I was in love with Jenn, and he urged me to ask her out "before someone else does." Just as I was working up my nerve to ask her to hang out, someone else *did*. Kevin was a six-foot-six surfer with rippling muscles and steel blue eyes. He was likable, but I wished he'd just go away.

Months into their relationship, Jenn and I went out as friends and drove. We headed to the North Shore, talked as we went west on Northern Blvd. and into Queens where I gave her a tour of my schools, playgrounds, former jobs, hangouts and stomping grounds. We hadn't had more of each other than a few minutes at a time until now and I learned volumes.

I don't know how I mustered the confidence—or maybe it was stupidity—but at one point, I told her that if she and Kevin didn't work out, I'd love to be with her. She fell silent for most of the rest of the ride and I imagined that I screwed up.

Within days, she told me she felt for me and we kissed. She and Kevin weren't getting along and within months *(it felt like years)* they'd broken up.

Jenn tells me that during the breakup Kevin made one request. He asked, "Whatever you do, promise me you won't date Seth."

We married three years later.

SING, 1993 - AGE TWENTY-EIGHT

AMONG THE PAYING gigs I had during the 90's, there existed a circuit of bookstores I'd rotate through every few months. When playing bars and clubs with a band, there would rarely be a dime left after the door guy and the sound guy and the split with other players. The lugging of equipment and the tension among band mates combined with my personal quirks (which included rarely being in tune and having trouble remembering forms) to make the whole effort a drag. I was unprofessional.

Being a solo artist was scary but had its appeal. I liked trying out new material or changing songs around, writing songs on the spot, and not having to worry that the band didn't know what I was about to do. There were the bars and cafés and odd clubs where I became a staple, but then several branches of Borders and of Barnes and Nobles had me play for a couple of hours, as would a few smaller independent book shops.

Folk music in Manhattan was making way for folk-punk hybrids where my music and me felt at home. I regularly played these "anti-folk" spots like The Sidewalk on Avenue A, The Speakeasy on MacDougal Street, and the Baggot Inn on W. 3rd, and even when the crowds came, it did not pay.

I love bookstores and the opportunity to spend time alone browsing, before or after set up and break down, somehow connected me and justified the erratic turnout and overall absurdity of the gigs. The audiences were made up of some people on my mailing list and then at times the crowd would grow as shoppers came upon a pleasant sound and had a little time to kill.

At first I got paid by check, $200 plus coffee or food for two to three hours, with breaks. As time went on, budgets—and appreciation—for entertainment got smaller, and so did my checks. Eventually, I'd play for $50 and a store gift card, and soon just a gift card. I would grab up some new books or CD's after my performance, order a hot chocolate, and thank my lucky starts that I got to play music. After a while though, the diminishing pay added to my souring taste for my chosen artistic path.

These gigs are a specific kind of hell, where there are few or no people present, or there is a crowd but none of them are listening. There's the blatant rudeness or drunk fuck disrespect that you come to expect at bars, but then there's the simple fact that people often go to clubs or bars or cafes or festivals to hang out with their friends, to meet people, and not always to hear music. I couldn't really blame them.

A working musician is not always playing a feature and these audiences sometimes care as much about a live singer as they do about a jukebox. The bookstores are ambitious in pursuit of planning events that will be cool and culturally rich, but sometimes the only people in attendance are book patrons. A solo musician is a curious guest and a noisy one at that.

Around this time, I developed the habit of closing my

eyes when singing, telling myself that it would make it easier to get really intimate with my song. I feel my guitar against my torso. I imagine that I'm at a larger venue and I have everyone's attention and everyone is receiving my gift, the way it's supposed to happen.

It was at one such appearance in a large bookstore in Bayside, Queens, that I found myself at my designated side of the store at show time, a dozen or so rows of chairs lined up neatly. On this rainy and air conditioned evening I began my set with a handful of occupied seats and when I opened my eyes in between songs I saw fewer faces and then each time I would reopen my eyes I'd silently react to the cruel game of musical chairs these strangers played with delicate me. I began to realize that I close my eyes, not just to plug into my song, but also to hide—to get away from what seeing rejection and disinterest does to a soul whose only desire is to connect. I realized that I would miss out on the deep stare and the opportunity to see someone really connecting, but that I'd also miss the chatting, yawning, the looking away, and the host of other goings-on which distract me and which I tend to take way too personally.

I also wondered how I continued to do this to myself, and for how long I should go on before admitting that it was all a lie, that my mother was right and I should have been a lawyer or married rich. That I should have picked an art earlier, and decided, and focused, and studied, and tried, to be the best at something instead of diluting my energy on so many different things, and being merely good instead of very good or excellent at one. That my fuckhead oldest first cousin, who laughed when I told him I was going to be a musician and didn't even RSVP for my wedding, was right. That what mattered the most to me was actually an elusive and juvenile dream.

Now, beyond thoughts of how I could dull the pain and make sure it never returned, relief that had been in the forefront of my obsessions for as long as I could remember, I was another kind of *done*. I was done wasting my time with art that would never work. This would be my last night *ever, ever, ever,* playing for anyone. I was leaving. Fuck you all. I'd go be normal and figure it out or not, but I wouldn't want to die every time I played anymore, and I wouldn't play for anyone. I was done with the trap of being sort of good or, perhaps great but still doomed to a talent "pool" where I was fucking drowning. I was leaving. Many years and hundreds of gigs and loads of songs and millions of miles all put before my health, my friends, my family and before any real and responsible plan for a future where I wouldn't be doomed to the same thing again and again.

I had long suspected—and feared—but on this night I decided that this was a waste of my life. Pain like this is rare and pain like this had grown cold inside me before, every time, in fact, that I had considered NOT making art. It was a trap, a Catch 22, *squared.* It was my curse.

And I minded my watch and I was professional and I resolved to finish and I dug into the last song of my set. The last song I'd ever play to a room full of passers-by. The pathetic last song that would ever be confused as programmed music playing over the stores' speakers because no one looks up anymore. Because people just don't give a shit about art or heartbreak or redemption or love unless it's being presented by someone who's hot, famous, or dead.

And the words to the song that had once mattered to me were not just syllables and sound and instead reminded me that I was sad and there was grief in the voice that sang loud and flat and I was bathed in the tragedy that was being proposed by my shame and my frustration. Something about drawing lines with chalk in the rain and about climbing an endless hill and more shit like that.

And I recalled Mom telling me that I could not be an artist for work, and I knew she was small and wrong, but I was programmed nonetheless and I hated her once again, and there was no way around this, and so I sang loud and I sang the chorus again and I tasted a tear. I didn't even know I was crying and as happened only a fraction of the time, I was present and I sang the chorus just one more time.

The song wound down and I was listening, a witness to a story for the sake of a story, a song for the sake of a song. I am a singer because I sing.

And I finished and stayed for a few seconds in my darkness and then I opened my eyes and there were people standing at the back looking on, and there were more people standing to the sides and a few crouched in front of book cases and others watching from behind.

There were three young ladies, maybe twenty to twenty-five years old in the front center; only twelve feet from me and the two on the ends had their arms around the one in the middle. She was shaking with some powerful hurt, and the other two joined her in her sobs, and they were looking at me as if we had been talking about their heartbreak and not mine. Then this room full of fuck-heads who don't care suddenly cared and they clapped. *Because they had listened. Because I had played.*

I was confused. And I was clear. And I still close my eyes. *And I still sing.*

BLAME, 1994 - AGE TWENTY-NINE

I USED TO blame my parents for my difficulties, ranging from poverty and poor diet habits to bigotry and despicable modeling. It's gotten immensely better but I'm still tempted to go there. This is not reasonable. Lots of people overcome. Lots of people *will* themselves to be a clean slate. Lots of people do actually consider themselves successful, and therefore have no need to find someone else to blame. Or they *own* their failure.

My mother always told me never to talk to neighbors about money, that it was none of anyone's business. People could not be trusted. I complied, knowing that she was hiding my dad's illness and corresponding unemployability, our debt, our welfare checks. My own shame existed as a natural state. I was always weird and interpreted others glances as judgments, true or not. I still do sometimes.

I didn't begin to specifically hate the fact that we were poor until kids began to make fun of me. This was a New York City housing project where no one was doing very well, but as cruelty comes naturally to little boys, a few of them began to single me out and make fun of our situation.

They'd see my dad's Plymouth Duster, older and rustier and any other car on the block. The one that mom made him park at least a block away from restaurants or social events so that no one would put *her* and *it* together.

They'd seen us walking home from the community

center carrying provisions, like Government Cheese. We qualified, some didn't.

So added to *"monkey-face"* and *"Jew"* we now had *"Seth's on welfare."* Oh, and the fun made of my too short pants, *"Where's the flood?."*

I knew that however much I hated it, my parents hated it more; my dad in a quiet, self loathing glaze, my mom ever shocked by missing her boat, marrying the wrong guy and living beneath her taste in trendy neighborhoods and artful things. She and I would walk up and down Austin Street in nearby Forest Hills and enjoy fantasies of living in a beautiful place, of having nice things. She took me to museums in the city and told me why Picasso was great, how Lautrec had suffered, and she made good on her promise to show me the techniques that were the trademarks of Seurat. She craved a life full of art and meaning, away from the roaches and the conflict.

Myself, I couldn't keep money. I'd insist on picking up the tab and tipping a little too well rather than splitting the bill, and going home with a few extra bucks. It was the same with drugs. As soon as I took possession of a resource I'd go for the immediate buzz of spending, ingesting and sharing.

My mom said, "You need to make a lot of money." That hypocritical mantra changed, once she began to quote Bernard Meltzer, the AM radio guru of everything practical. Then she said "It's not what you earn, it's what you save." She always said to go into computers," computers are gonna be hot." Be a lawyer or a doctor. You can't do music for a living. I have suffered unduly for considering this. Do it on the side, but be a doctor. Or, she finally decided, marry rich.

In late 1988, during my second year clean, I moved in with Jackie. Her dad was a wealthy real estate developer and my parents felt as if I'd hit the lottery. Jackie was a smart, pretty, spoiled, and overly tanned twenty-one year old rebel with a Porsche, a Maserati, and a deviated septum. She tried to mold me and screamed at me that my parents raised me wrong. The anger I felt at this remark remained at my side, ready to fuel many subsequent fights.

We put off our breakup as long as we could, conspiring to delay the pain that would inevitably follow, but we were killing each other with epic philosophical and personal debates. She was so used to getting what she wanted, and I was sure that I never would. She wanted me to be refined. I wanted her to be nice.

I moved out in a "trial" separation, agreeing that time apart would seal the gashes in our hearts and we'd get back together in a few months. Then, speaking to her from a phone booth near my new apartment fifty miles away, she told me it was over and I freaked out and asked her to marry me, which is what she'd wanting for me to say in the first place. She said that it was too late. I'm so glad it didn't work out. She had a boyfriend waiting. I think she married him. I do hope she's happy.

When I told my parents that we'd broken up I could sense their dismay and I felt guilty, like I'd failed or failed them. Then my father, never one to use discretion, blurted out his truth: "She's *stupid!* She shouldn't be mean to you." My mother couldn't summon anything approaching support, but she kept quiet.

Sitting at my parent's dinette table after returning back from a doctor's appointment, we were talking about my music, and she was asking good questions and being happy and supportive. Then again she said something about it never working out and having to have real employment in order to survive, and more of the fear stuff. In truth, she wasn't wrong. But I was immediately angry at her for dismissing my heart's desires, and all the hard work I'd put in, but also for how she had vacated her own happy place in favor of fear and insecurity.

I was fed up for many reasons, but they all came out in this exchange. I told her that my collective failures to that point were because of what she'd taught me. That she needed to stop continually asserting that money needed to come before passion, or that they had to be separate. She knew nothing, and was the product of her own limiting beliefs. She'd messed me up in many ways and this might have been the biggest. Her poverty-speak had affected me in incurably negative ways. That part of why I kept finding myself destitute and why I'd never given my music and my art a full shot was because of reservations that *she* had planted in my brain. I was a loser and her bullshit was to blame.

She heard me out.

She was quiet and breathed controlled breaths a few times then frowned big and spoke through clenched teeth.

"Sit down."

I sat.

"When I was a little girl, no one could get a job. My mother stood over my father. He was sitting at the table with his face in his hands. And my mother yelled into his face, *we need food!* Go ... get ... *FOOD!*"

She went on to tell me how her dad cried in frustration, as there was no money to be made during the depression, no food to be gotten. How her family had always struggled and how they went without. And how she and my dad hadn't had it much easier but had managed to have food, if not much else.

She told me that she worries about me, and that she didn't want me to suffer the way she had. She told me that she didn't know any other way and that she was trying to help me, not hurt me. She told me that I should cut it out. She was livid and she was clear. And suddenly, she was right.

Any effort to talk my way free of the rules I'd learned so many years before was wasted. It was as if we now both saw the trap that had been laid, understood its intended usefulness, and that although it might have no business here and now, it would not change. I felt for Mom and I know she felt for me. Neither of us had the will to rewrite the story, and my pessimism deepened.

FIRE

ACT 1.

IT'S **1981** AND I steal my brother's 1962 AMC Rambler and set it on fire in a parking lot under the Throng Neck Bridge in Queens. The circumstances are dire and while I know that I'm breaking the law—along with my brothers heart—and destroying a thing of beauty, I'm driven, and I think I'm doing the right thing, an *excellent* thing, in fact. As I drive off in the back seat of my friends Trans-Am, a1981 Daytona 500 pace car, I look back at the culmination of my brothers big dream, now burning orange, green, and blue in the foreground of the Throgs Neck Bridge. I *know* that I've gone too far, and that I will never live this down. I know that although I've temporarily solved one problem, I've created others.

ACT 2

IT'S **1995** AND at seven a.m., I'm already at work. I'm in the kitchen and stressed out about—among other things—the condition of our overheating 1986 Plymouth Voyager, which has over 160,000 miles on it, a slipping transmission, a quart-a-day oil habit, and a curse. Jeff was going to fix it today but when I drove the smoking beast past his makeshift shop in the automotive repair shanty-town by the oil refinery in Oceanside at our agreed upon time this morning, Jeff was not there. He'd assured me that it would be fixed today but now I'm sick again with that very particular kind of sick that my mind and body reserve just for car issues, the nausea that takes over every cell in my body when the engine light goes on or a new grinding sound emits from under the hood because I know that I don't have the money to get it fixed, and that there is foolishness and abuse inherent in the non-fixing and the associated shame and helpless resignation. Jenn says *Seth! The car's on fire!* I run to the front of the store and see black smoke rising from under the car and flames dancing around the front tires. Cars veer into the parking lot as Good Samaritans—en route to their respective jobs—stop, grab their fire extinguishers and begin to do what they can. I lose dozens of books, cassettes, a treasured pair of baggy corduroys, a platform bed I'd built in the back for the half year trek across country we recently returned from, and the car. Covered in soot but surviving are speaker stands and a mike stand. I'm usually the one calming Jenn down in stressful moments, but I feel completely ashamed and defeated and begin to cry. She starts to laugh. My car burns—orange, green, and blue. She asks if I can't see the humor in the situation and puts her hands on my soggy cheeks.

No. *I'm afraid I can't.*

Go Away, 1998 - AGE TWENTY-EIGHT

MY BIG BROTHER wanted to hear me play. He was always proud of me and brought a friend to my show, and a different friend to another show. They were similarly unsavory characters, each nice to me—and good people— but all clearly messed up. He introduced me as a musical genius *(I'm not)*. He said he taught me my first guitar chords *(he did)*. He said that I excelled at everything I do *(I never have)*. Kim said that even though he was older, I could kick his ass, but that I shouldn't try *(I had)*. He kissed me a lot in front of his friends, people I didn't know.

When we were introduced, though, there was an instant, unspoken bond. It was as if we were both saying "you poor fucking thing." Kim acted in a bizarre manner and blew all his money on payday dope, eating out, and showing off. He was inevitably broke and broken within a day.

That was when he would die again. He'd be dead to our father and dead to whomever he had befriended or tricked into believing that there could be anything but despair lying ahead in their pairing. Dead to his red Eldorado dreams, and to a woman named Joni who would make him whole, stitch up his heart and give his devil a chill pill. (They haven't spoken in twenty years).

I knew he was sensitive and as we had a psychic-brother-bond, I felt his pain. I *did* love him and I had been an asshole to him many times, so I was tolerant and thanked him for coming, although I really wished he'd have left.

I was nauseous, wondering how he was going to embarrass me *this* time. I wanted him to disappear. I sang my songs, unable to fully forget that my problem was just yards away, stealing the show; that my single greatest burden was right there. I would spend my life intervening and trying to keep him out of trouble. I was exhausted and distracted, partly because I was concerned about his welfare and partly because he was mooching from and destroying my parents. Now he just wouldn't shut the fuck up and I could hear him above all the amplified noise I'm making.

I closed my eyes and imagined an audience of strangers at the Bottom Line; listening and considerate as they consumed the musical feast I served. I checked back into my song. I was once again alive, connecting, and exactly where I was supposed to be. But then I heard the manic call of my name, the over-zealous clapping and the ordering another round.

It was so unprofessional, so unacceptable, pathetic and incredibly fucked up. It was never going to end. I was trapped. I wished he would go to rehab, or to Florida, or to jail. *Or just die already.*

BLEED, 1989 - AGE TWENTY-FOUR

JAY WAS THE person I called when Mom got her liver cancer diagnosis. I cried into the phone outside Booth Memorial Hospital and felt only slightly less alone. Jay had lost his mother while he was in college and had overcome adversity so gracefully; I just needed him in that moment. My mother would go into remission after this battle, and two years later, after her kidney got it's chance, but when her primary doctor, a renowned pulmonary specialist first detected her lung cancer, it had already metastasized.

She was scheduled for surgery and my dad and I waited in the over air-conditioned lounge for the news. When Dr. Masina emerged, he told us that she was doing well, that they'd removed a substantial mass, and that they'd attack the rest with rounds of chemo and radiation therapy.

He seemed a little too cheerful for the circumstances and I asked for a layman's determination of her condition. He hesitated for a few seconds then the arc of his smile straightened a bit. "She has stage four lung cancer. Treatments may keep her around longer, but there's no recovering." He said that we'd meet later to discuss a course of action, then squeezed my dad's arm, and shook my hand. I held onto it as I noticed the bandage wrapped around his other hand. "What happened there?"

He chuckled and said that he'd cut himself; and began to turn away. I asked him when the cut occurred. He said that it was during surgery, that he'd accidentally cut his finger while working on my mother, had tended to it and continued the procedure. He started to repeat that we'd convene later when I interrupted. *"Did you bleed into my mother?"* He laughed about it and tried to assure me that they'd handled it immediately and that there was no need for concern.

He left us to process things, the cancer for my dad, the cancer and the blood for me, the broken world for both of us. Dad didn't want to hear me mention the blood again; saying that he was a doctor, *dammit,* and he that he wouldn't do anything that would hurt Mom. He said that I was upset and angry and that I was looking for someone to blame, and that the doctor was on our side, to leave it alone.

The next day, I sat in a chair next to Mom's hospital bed helping her eat applesauce I'd brought from the health food store. I'd laced it with crushed up vitamin C and probiotics, and Dr. Messina walked in, smiling, Manila folder in hand. Mom always softened in his presence, charming and helpful as he always was. She asked how his finger was and he joked about the accident he'd had during surgery, saying something about being related now. He asked how Mom was feeling, cheerfully explained his prescribed course and schedule of action and turned to leave.

Smiling and in the calmest voice I could muster, I said, "Can we please see a blood test?" He assured me that Mom's blood was being monitored and asked if I was concerned with any particular studies. I told him that I wanted to see a report on *his* blood. Mom immediately said, "Oh, Seth," and laughed in embarrassment. The doctor said nothing, and for the first time ever, stopped smiling. It was ok for me to ask for this I assured her, and asked him again, saying that it seems irresponsible to me that he hadn't suggested it first.

A few days later, he took me in the hall and I trusted him when he told me that his full blood work up had come up with nothing contagious. I only said, "Good," and walked away. He deserved no thanks for doing the right thing and he offered no apology. At this point, I hated him. He was a lung specialist who saw Mom regularly and had missed her lung cancer at stages one, two and three. *Fuck him.*

I considered filing a malpractice suit to address this negligence (as well as the whole bleeding into my dying Mom and joking about it thing), but my parents talked me down. Her treatment would be hard on the whole family. I was driving Dad to his own doctor's appointments as well as trying in vain to manage Kim's crumbling life.

After a round of chemo, Mom was left feeling weak, nauseous, and hopeless. We met with the oncologist as the plan for the next few months was laid out. We discussed logistics, getting Dad around, and were directed to a social worker that would help us get necessary equipment for home as well as a visiting aide, if necessary. I brought them home and Dad sent me out for a Carvel ice cream cake. It was my birthday. As I overate, Mom said that she's made a decision. She didn't want to do any more treatment. She was not afraid of death, she said. She just didn't want to feel sicker than she needed to.

Already helpless, Dad didn't say a word. To me, this stand made her seem somehow powerful. Although she was saying what we all wanted to avoid at all costs, to put off for as long as possible, we now finally began the process of accepting the inevitable.

Dad and I, at least.

KIM, 2001 - AGE THIRTY-SIX

IT WAS HOT as hell on August 1, 2001, the day my brother came to help us move into our new apartment in Long Beach, the day my brother died.

Our building, 25 Franklin Blvd., was between the ocean and the rest of the world, into which we were now inching. There, in just about the most neglected building in the city, we'd met a few friends, rescued a handful of cats, had some parties and taught some cooking classes. I'd also made a record, which I was about to release, tour behind, and promote.

We were moving to a larger, better place on East Broadway, just one block north and two blocks west. There was a pool. I felt sad to leave the ocean. It would be only a short walk away now, but it felt like many miles.

They showed up hours late, and they were useless. My brother, Kim, was 5 foot-seven, powder-pale and jumpy. His friend, Angelo, was a giant, 6 foot-eight, black, and loud. If one didn't turn heads on the street, together they did.

I'd grown accustomed to seeing my brother as handicapped. That way I was able to keep from screaming at him and hating him for all the shit he was putting my parents through, and all the futile effort I'd put in—the detox, rehab, and emergency room trips, and dragging him to meetings. The headlocks and threats. He was weak

212

and spineless, and now his once-brilliant conversation was reduced to babbling. He couldn't make it across the room without wondering why he'd begun.

Kim driving a car scared the hell out of me. He'd lost his job driving a garbage truck. After his infrequent baths (he *hated* showers) he'd put on the same dirty clothes, so he always smelled. But his and Angelo's assistance was well intentioned, and I treated it as such. I had them follow me with a box or a frame a few times, before I began to grow impatient and feel the judgments of neighbors and passersby, their spectacle and discourse too hard to ignore. Although we had hours of work ahead of us, I told them to go grab lunch and check out the boardwalk. We had it covered, I said.

A long while later I assumed that they had just considered themselves dismissed. I ascended the ramp to the boardwalk and scanned the waves. Out in the surf, between the Neptune Boulevard jetty and the surfers, was a strange, fully dressed little man. Straight-faced, deep-chested, and garnering the attention of sunbathers, there were a few pointing children and a couple of laughing lifeguards.

I jumped down to the sand and walked toward him, flashing visions of him moving to this town, enjoying the beach, behaving himself, and getting a life. I had always hoped for his problems to dissolve so that we could enjoy one another as much as we loved one another. He walked to shore, then to the boardwalk, and I turned and walked beside him. "When was the last time you were in the ocean?" I asked. He looked straight ahead. "Thirty years."

I walked him to his car and along the way we found sweaty, overheated Angelo, who had gone wandering as well. The extent of physical exertion these two were accustomed to had long been limited to the balancing act their bodies had to wage against their massive chemical consumption. Their exposure to this heat wave and fresh air concerned me.

Kim opened his trunk to expose an incredible mess. He took out the CD copy of my record, my first, which I had given him the week before at a show he'd come out to—I wished he hadn't—and pointed to the picture on the back cover. It was me at three or four, posing with my hands and mouth on my brother's tenor saxophone. The sax is as tall I am, and I'm standing it on the floor and looking like I'm about to wail. My brother is 14 or so, standing shirtless in the background, hands overhead on the low-hanging chin-up bar, and he's smiling. There's a Dylan poster on the door next to him. It's a beautiful moment. When designing the artwork with my friend, I suggested we make the little kid in the picture more prominent and find a way to slightly obscure the big kid. I just thought it might look cool. So Chris blurred the part of the picture where my brother stood, and it did look cool, and we used it.

My brother pointed to the picture and said, "You don't blur me out of out of pictures. I'm your big brother and you shouldn't be ashamed of me. Do you understand?" I began to explain that it was a strictly aesthetic decision and that it actually features him. I told that I meant no disrespect. But the truth was that during the time I had worked on the project, and for years leading up to it, the living, breathing Kim already was obscured. I had been furious with him. I was really done with him, and that had fed my decision. There was a part of me that imagined a world without him, one in which he had already died and in which I was freed from the ugly obligations. I hadn't considered how he might have felt about this, and at the time I truly hadn't cared.

But now I cared. "I'm sorry," I said, promising I'd fix any subsequent printings to include an unobscured picture of him and me. "Ok," he said. "I love you and I love Jenn and I love the cats." And, like that, he forgave me. Then we hugged and he left.

My brother had driven a garbage truck for the city. He would tell me about the different sized dumpsters, and the power he felt lifting these immovable giants of urban purging. There was clearly a sense of accomplishment when driving away from a site, having made room for the residents and the businesses to carry on because he had been called. It was a far cry from his rookie years when he'd clean out South Bronx alleys by rake and hand. There, he had been gashed by broken glass and stuck by hypodermic needles carelessly tossed into plastic trash bags. He once had a crack-head's box cutter at his throat, just because. In the same South Bronx where by night he'd eventually cop dope, where he'd engage the gutters to fool his heart and to numb his conscience.

I am an addict, although I don't use drugs any more.

Seth Branitz

I stopped getting high when I was twenty-two. In the challenging months that followed, I embarked on a sort of reinvention. I needed to be clean. I needed to do away with any and all of my default thoughts and impulses. They had led me to the edge, where I had teetered since I first got addicted to coke at sixteen. They had only solidified my notions of worthlessness and irreconcilable shame, which had been with me since childhood. Once I got clean, I avoided the places where I'd used and acquired my drugs. I hid from those with whom I'd used, and I tried very hard to brace myself for my very infrequent visits with my family. These were the most consequential of my interactions in my first years among the living. There was the same darkness that drugs had helped me to hide from, except now the pain that I'd attempted to dull for so long was up front-and-center. On top of the needs my parents imposed on me, my brother's dysfunction had ramped up to a level of abuse. He abused their space and took from them. They abused him psychologically and verbally. They hated him, and he lived in their space, craving connection and desperate for validation, but inadvertently hating them back. There was no hope because everyone felt wronged and everyone was hurt. It was fucking impossible, but I kept trying to save him from them, and them from him.

Until and unless an addict is ready and willing to grow up, we all have to rationalize our wrongs. We blame someone else or we blame our unfortunate lot. We compare ourselves to another, saying, "At least I'm not *that* bad." And maybe we're right, but that won't save us. My brother's last remnant of decency lay in that truck. It was his power. His one-up on murderers, homeless people, litterbugs and losers. It was also his boyhood Tonka toy, all grown up.

I'd experienced the progression of hard drug use first-hand, beginning in my teens. I'd cried in utter helplessness and lamented the waste of my own gift each and every time I reached for another hit. Every lie hurt. And the pain merely changed at the start of my own recovery. I'd felt it drag me down and leave me bankrupt—emotionally, spiritually, physically—and then watched as friends continued on to their inevitable institutionalizations, incarcerations, and graves. I mourned suicides, homicides, AIDS and unrecognizable victims in the shells of daughters and sons who'd once shown promise. Once I'd wiggled free from the noose I wove daily through my entire adolescence and into my twenties, I watched as my brother fell deeper.

I'd accompanied him to shrinks and had dragged him to meetings, and on multiple occasions he asserted that he was going to stop. He wanted to live. He wanted for us to grow old together. Then fucking Nicky or Bill would call and ask for a ride to cop. Dad would stomp on his confidence and no amount of space could quiet the shame. His junk-soaked blood and brain would agonize for more.

"You don't have to live this way," I said again and again.

"I like the way I live," he lied.

"You're killing Mom and Dad."

"They killed me a long time ago."

"Kim, you can be happy again."

"I've NEVER BEEN HAPPY!"

And so in a life absent of happiness, overflowing with grief—in desperate, futile attempts to quiet the bloodied army in his mind—he used more.

Jenn and I went to sleep in our new apartment at 333 E. Broadway that night, drained from the long day of lugging our stuff in the brutal heat. Around midnight, she woke me. "It's your mom," she said "Something's wrong with Kim." I had slept right through the phone ringing.

"Seth ... " Mom's terrified voice rang. They'd been called by the hospital. "Kim's in the hospital and they won't tell me anything. They need someone to go there." I kept cool for her and got the number of the doctor who'd called her.

He was intense, even as he told me, "Yes, you have to come here."

"What's wrong," I asked, and he said he wasn't allowed to give me any information, that a family member had to come there.

"Can you at least tell me if he's alive?" I asked.

"I can't tell you anything. You *have* to come to the hospital," was all he could offer.

Jenn said she would come along and I told her that there was no need for both of us to lose sleep. There was nothing she could do. I'd just call her and let her know once I got there. She squinted at me as if to say, "Are you fucking kidding me?" She put her sneakers on and we headed for the door.

We drove to Lincoln Hospital in The Bronx in virtual

silence. The possible scenarios flipped through my mind as I tried to secure some control over what was likely to be a completely hopeless circumstance.

My brother's junkie friend, Angelo, greeted us outside the E.R. and said he was going to get some answers. Kim was fine. I should just sit tight. All under control. He was very warm and big brotherly. That's how most of my brother's friends used to treat me.

I asked for the doctor by name. A nurse came from behind the counter, and we were escorted to a small conference room off of the regular waiting room. As we turned to follow, Jenn whispered, "Shit." We squeezed our held hands tightly as we walked to the room.

We passed through the doorway and I heard Angelo's voice and the African accent of the doctor I'd spoken to on the phone. The doctor was saying he couldn't talk with him and then Angelo getting loud. Intense, loud whispers, then Angelo screaming. A big grieving man scream: *"KIMM . . . NOOO KIMMMM!!"* This is how I found out.

With Angelo crying loudly in the background, and the sound of something pounding—Angelo's fist? His feet stomping? The doctor came and explained that the reason that he could not tell me anything on the phone was because my brother was, indeed DEAD.

"I'm very sorry," he said. We both kept wincing in reaction to Angelo's fit. This poor young doctor had tears in his eyes. I'd just lost my brother—for good this time—and I was sad for him. *What a job.* We embraced. I asked the doctor if we could see my brother. A nurse led us through the emergency room, where another nurse made a sassy comment to ours. Our nurse responded with wide open "shut-the-fuck-up" eyes, and the other, now aware of why we were there, shut the fuck up and just kept on walking.

A rolling bed guarded a closed curtain behind which lay my only brother. We stood over him and I said I was sorry, and then kissed him on his clammy forehead. I loved his face, and ran my hand across his head, breathing in the smell of smoke and sweat. I resisted trying to get a handle on this, my most surreal moment to date. I looked at Jenn. We hugged and we left.

A couple of days later the retirement-age city coroner would tell me that his autopsy showed that any individual quantity of the cocaine, alcohol, and heroin that Kim had ingested that day would have killed him. She said that it was clear that he was a "career addict."

We left the hospital, in shock, sometime after 3 a.m. After making our first right, glistening in the light of a lamppost— the only sign of life for blocks—was a New York City Department of Sanitation rear-loading garbage truck. *It takes a long time to understand that someone has died.* I'd had mere minutes to begin assigning meaning to coincidence and began seeing signs everywhere. This truck was a steel and hose barrel-chested angel with wings outstretched and bound for eternity. I wanted to stop the car and board the truck, or to just watch it. Maybe my brother would climb out of the cab and come to our car and I'd cry through tears of relief. Maybe he'd give me a tour of the truck he had bragged about so many times. Maybe he'd let me move the lever and crush something. I wanted to be proud of my brother. I wanted him back. On this block, in this hellhole, my brother hadn't yet died.

The worst hadn't come. We drove on through the night to Queens on a mission to tell my parents their child was dead.

When someone who needs help doesn't accept it, you become infuriated, and then you become resigned. But when the consequences of *their* trespasses become *your* consequences and they just lie, ruin and avoid, in the face of what has become your sacrifice, then hatred brews.

I hated my brother for sure, but I adored him and would have done anything to bring him peace, to rescue him. I'd recently told him once again that if he'd just go through detox, stop hanging out with losers, go to meetings, begin doing the things that happy people do, then he could have a nice life.

I'd called the Sanitation Department's Employee Assistance Unit to get clear on the help that could be available to those who needed it. They could have set him up with paid leave, rehab and outpatient therapy. When I reiterated the promising news to my brother he freaked out. "Are you fucking kidding me? You want me to go to the Employee Assistance Unit; to my job and tell them I'm a drug addict?" He was furious that I'd called on his behalf. I had done so anonymously, of course, but there was no calming his paranoia. Once, when he confided his remorse to me, I saw a window to his humility and told him I would arrange detox and rehab for him and we could go that very day. Through his tears, he asked if they'd let him use heroin there.

Now he was dead. There would be no more of his bullshit. Forget that I, the younger brother, had been the more responsible one for half of our lives together and that he'd been my consuming nightmare. I'd lost my one and only sibling.

The ride to my parents' apartment in Flushing happened like one of those sleeps that last an entire night but feel like mere seconds has passed. There were blurred store signs, muted police sirens, minimal words, and terror. How were we to compose ourselves for a task like this? What could we do?

There must be a protocol for comforting the dying, as my mother was. Like just being there. Just being a sounding board or holding a space open for them to process their process, while reminding them that sunshine is still lovely and humor still feels good, if only for now. But this new development twisted reality in a most cruel and impossible way.

I was a wet ton as I lifted myself out of the car and walked toward my parents' building. I'd never wanted to run away more than I did right then. I wanted to just drive off into oblivion. I have friends who live hundreds of miles away from the nearest city in New Mexico, and we could just show up and live with them, catch water, make mud bricks and sleep in a tent with dogs that would guard our perimeter from the howling coyotes at night. I wanted so badly to be free.

I felt horrible for dragging Jenn into this, but she took it on as if it were *her* own family, *her* own brother, *her* duty. She'd lost her big sister a decade earlier, and had a sense of strength here that kept us focused on this thing.

In the elevator there was no more running. "Are you sure you're up for this?" I asked. She nodded and did not ask me the same question. Of course I wasn't. We got out, made a right turn and walked the horrible walk to their door, unlocked it and went in.

"How's Kim?" my mother asked. "Is he ok?" I looked at her blankly. *"Is he dead?"* I stood there. *"DEAD!? Honey! Honey! He's dead! Kim! Our Kim!"* Mom screamed. She would have run around the apartment if her cancer had left her any strength.

Dad slumped into shock. *"YOU DID THIS,"* Mom yelled at the father who had just lost his son. *"You always hated him!"*

"It's no one's fault, Mom. Please let's not make it worse."

In a while, the panic subsided. We commenced our mourning with two hours in my parents' bedroom. We were going to stay over, or at least I was, but my mom said, "Go home. You should sleep. I'm okay."

Throughout all their years of neediness, their dependence, and the demands of their respective conditions, I had complied, not always willingly. And throughout, they apologized. They'd say things like, "This is too much for

223

you," or "I'm not sure how you're doing this."

I felt used and overextended beyond my limit. I had explained away and advocated for them since I was young, and thought I must be cursed to have such a desperate and pathetic family. But I'd say, "It's no big deal." or "You had *me* ... this is nothing."

The following day I got my crash course in making funeral arrangements. I'd plan two more in the coming months, and through them all, as one-by-one I buried my entire immediate family, I maintained a tense detachment. I called one cousin and asked her to call the others. I asked one of my friends to call whomever they thought should know. I did the same with my mom's friends. Dad had none to speak of, but I did print up a small sign and posted it between the two elevators in the lobby of their building.

"The funeral for Kim Branitz will be at ..."

My dad kept telling me he couldn't go. My mom kept splitting off into semi-cheerful idle talk and then into supreme darkness, then back. We each dealt with this loss our in own way. The guilt was heaviest for them, as I had shown up as fully as I could have, given my brother's insufferable unwillingness to be supported in recent years. Our parents had continued to give him shit for everything, yet continued providing room and board regardless of his unwavering trail of destruction. They did this knowing it wouldn't help, that nothing would help. But they couldn't bear turning him out to the streets where he looked and smelled like he lived. True, my mom was now dying from her cancer. And Dad's heart was leaking, and there was this test that was going to tell us if the doctor's suspicion was correct about leukemia. He had been taking mom's painkillers and some days could barely get out of bed. Their bodies were already a mess, but Kim's death definitely killed them.

If, on the other hand, Kim had lived, Mom's death was something he couldn't have borne. A few months earlier, I attempted to have a conversation with him about accountability, and the importance of getting clean, and ending the barrage of problems he brought home to our suffering parents. I realized that he didn't have an understanding of mom's prognosis and I thought it imperative for him to know. "Kim, Mommy's dying," I said. "You do realize that, don't you?"

He sulked deeply, and then exploded. *"Fuck you! You're MEAN!"* He couldn't even look at me. He nearly head-butted me as he lashed his second *"FUCK YOU!,"* delivered through a distorted frown that took over his whole face and his entire body. A few weeks later Mom told me that Kim had been crying inconsolably in bed one day, and when she sat with him and rubbed his back and asked what was wrong, he said that I had told him that she was dying. He was angry with me for saying such a thing. He fucking told on me. Imagine dying Mom, consoling her grown son, in denial over her own impending death, then her bringing it to me. It was really fucked up. She wasn't mad at me, just telling me. She and I were very, very close.

My brother was pathetic.

So we mourned. For the few-hours-long Shiva, in the dark, cluttered apartment my parents shared with him, there were many pictures of Kim in better times. He had been the most beautiful child. I heard myself saying how perfect he was and still cannot bear the tragedy, the waste.

And now I write, not to forget (I'll never forget) but to maybe put this great expanse of spoiled fortune on a high shelf. Set it aside for small bits of time. To know it's there and that I can take it out now and then and make a little more sense out of it if I feel up for the challenge. When I feel strong enough to know it won't kill me.

It didn't the first time.

Psych, 2002 - AGE THIRTY-SIX

MY PARENTS WERE dependent on an assortment of pills during my entire childhood. People used to get older sooner, and they were moving toward old as long as I can remember. Dad was forty when I was born, and I always recall his teeth in a glass cup on the bathroom counter. Hospitals, doctors, arthritis, grey hair, shrinks and pills.

In early 2002, over a year after my mother's terminal prognosis and just weeks after my brother's fatal overdose, Dad himself overdosed on my Mom's antidepressants and ended up at LI Jewish Hospital. Once his vitals were steady—except for the clear and present danger presented by congestive heart failure—one cardiologist got pale during Dad's examination and told him to just go ahead and eat anything that he wanted, to enjoy his life; it was time to go home. He wanted to get to my mom so he could do whatever he could to comfort her and take care of her. Getting home to her was all he had to motivate him. His body was a bag of broken pieces and his mind, a dark pit of resignation. He was transferred to the psychiatric ward, instead.

The other patients there were in more advanced stages of crazy. They ranged from constantly screaming, to steadily drooling. My father looked around in horror and said that he didn't belong there. This was true. There was no rehabilitation to be had here for someone with my dad's particular group of afflictions. I advocated for him, vying for the undivided ear of overburdened early-career social workers and therapists, explaining why this was too much and how he really did need to go home.

The staff psychotherapist would come by daily and check in on my dad. He begged to go home, but because he was a suicide risk, they had concerns that ranged from the real to the litigious. I can only imagine what he said in my absence, but during one consultation, the doctor asked if he was feeling better about life. Dad's malaise turned to contempt. "Feel better about life? Haven't you been paying attention? My son is dead. My wife is sick and alone at home and I *need* to get home and I'm here surrounded by nuts. How am I *supposed* to feel about life?"

Given all the sad details, this would likely have sufficed to justify a discharge, but Dad was honest and topped off the short discussion with, "I keep on looking over there and I'm gonna throw myself through that window." His eyes filled with rage and he turned to me and said, "What the fuck *is* this?" I tried to speak for him and explained the dire circumstance, that he's understandably upset and appropriately depressed, but that he's doing better and ready to head home as soon as she gives the ok. She regrouped and asked dad a few questions, ending, as usual, with, "Do you have any thoughts about hurting yourself?" He coolly and quietly responded, "Not today, but I do have thoughts about hurting *you.*"

This exchange sums it all up, what life is like with a crazy person who might not get better. Someone who, despite what you see is appropriate, possible, and right under their noses, will keep on presenting new and better ways to fuck everything up.

Once when he was short of breath, he called for a doctor. I intercepted a middle aged Indian doctor before he came in the room to prep him for Dad's emotional state. He was very empathetic and came into the room, charming and warm. A minute into his examination, my dad looked up at him and said, "Why are *you* here? Isn't this a *Jewish* hospital?"

When he finally got home, he spent almost all of his hours in bed. Proximity to Mom and the few times a day he brought her a drink made being there the most important thing.

Then he began to fall.

Break, 2001 -AGE THIRTY-SIX

WE HADN'T FALLEN out of love; we just didn't have any time *for* love. Our lives had been filled with non-stop crises what with my brother's suicide, caring for my aged, ill and depressed parents. Even when I *did* sleep at home, my wife and I would be interrupted by a phone call from the psych hospital where dad spent weeks at a time, or from Mom—living out her third cancer at home, on hospice—saying that dad had fallen, or that he'd taken her pain meds, or that he wasn't waking up. They need me. Please come.

My marriage had defaulted to a lower position of priority, and hoping to make up for lost time, to give our unromantic union a jump start, and to remind her of how it had once been—of hope for our future—I'd perused a couple of books on igniting sexual fire, one entitled *The Passionate Marriage,* and the other, a more playful text called *101 Nights of Great Sex.* There were many suggestions, some mild, some far out. I decided on a striptease.

I procured a pair of very small neon green briefs and rehearsed a few times in my head. I sat her down in front of the couch one late night, lit a few candles, shut the light and said to wait there. I left the room, changed into this sparse costume and hit play. Brian Ferry, Avalon. Around the corner I came.

Fighting back giggles I swayed and shimmied my way up to her, now peeking through fingers that were covering

230

her eyes, her gleeful, contorted smirk.

I slowly rubbed my chest and stupidly shook my ass, got down on the floor beside her, began to kiss her hair, her neck, her cheek. Our collective vulnerability began to transform as we felt fun, warm, safe, hot ...

Then the phone rang.

The phone kept ringing. Every muscle in both of our bodies tightened and I kept on kissing her. I had said these certain four words before in my life, like when I came face to face with my freshly expired brother, when I'd run out of drugs, when I'd had a gun in my back, and when I'd watched the smoke plume from the wreckage of the towers.

"This is *not* happening. *This is NOT happening.*"

"Seth. Seth. It's Mom. I'm sorry to bother you again. Dad fell. I can't get him up, Seth. I don't know what to do. Please call me back. Please."

I felt that if I stayed totally still, if I stopped breathing, if I ignored the obvious, that maybe it would go away, or that I could delay the pain.

"When are you going to break," my wife had regularly been asking me. "You've *got* to break. No one can just keep on showing up with what you're going through." I'd responded that I wasn't going through anything. This was *their* suffering—you know—*their* problems. I was just showing up for *them.*

I *had* to think this way in order to carry on. There was work to be done.

But there on the floor next to the light of dim flames,

incense wafting, and the medicine I'd conjured for my ailing marriage now smashed and running muddy in the gutter on this block of impossible sorrow, I was fucking beat. I had nothing left.

When I finally exhaled, the glue holding me up, holding me frozen in time snapped, and I became limp, my head falling into her lap. I sobbed. She held me and rocked me and we were so sad, so trapped on this carousel of burden. *Too dizzy to even step off.*

I cried for a bit. She put her hands on my shoulders, her forehead to mine and said, "Go, you have to go." Now when I stood up, wiped out, snot running, stupid little fucking green briefs, I felt old, and ugly, ashamed and betrayed—and loved.

I got dressed and kissed her good night.

I went, not choosing one love over another, but nurtured in the arms of both.

In collusion with love.

In debt to love.

In the service of love.

DREAM JOURNAL: SELECT ENTRIES

THIS IS A record of some nightmares I had during the worst of this ordeal from a notebook I kept next to my bed. I thought they might fit well here and there between stories ... not sure.

Some of this was very difficult to write. I'd moved past the acute stings of these events but the pain hadn't gone away. Revisiting the darkest moments gave me nightmares.

Last night/this morning I dreamed that my brother called me on the phone and asked when I would be home. He and my parents were waiting. It was getting late. I knew I'd be awhile, feeling all the guilt. I told him that.

Last night I had a dream that I'm parking my dad's car, a 1962 Ford Falcon on a side block at the corner of Queens Boulevard in Forest Hills. I'm running from shop to shop and not sure what I'm supposed to be getting but I keep looking. I'm going to fail. Mom will be pissed off and I will not have a good reason for failing her.

I cross the very large boulevard and see that the car is not there. Towed. No cops. More confusion.

Again I'll fail mom and drive dad deeper into crazy, deeper into debt to pay to get the car back. I cannot figure out how to contact the impound lot and don't want to go home, except I do want to go home. *But I can't.*

Seth Branitz

I had a dream that I'm on top of my brother on the ground and screaming at my brother and he's cursing at me and I begin punching him in the face and he keeps on cursing at me, *"fuck you!"* And I keep punching. His face begins to collapse under my fist and I keep on punching and crushing him, bones breaking and blood pooling on his distorted head. I've gone too far but it's too late.

Last night I dreamed that I was in apartment 4-A in Pomonok, the project where I lived from 1969-1987. Mom is cleaning up a dinner mess in the tiny kitchen and it's very late at night. I go into my bedroom and the trundle bed is pulled, raised, and made, and I go into my bed next to my brother, who's reading under the knit blanket grandma Ethel made. Everyone is alive and it feels like home.

I dreamed that I'm with my mother on a bench outside. We're both crying with love for my kids—her grandsons. She's in a nightgown, hunched in pain as I remember her. We're sharing their faces—their laughter, their uniqueness—with our minds.

Last night I dreamed that I was driving my dad's car, the Dart, I think. It was a long, straight road like Woodhaven Boulevard toward the Rockaways, and I suddenly see that the road is blocked by orange and white barricades, but I cannot stop and I crash through and then I'm in the air, falling, falling, and as I fall toward the water, my fate and the car's are certainly in jeopardy, all I think is "dad's gonna kill me."

The Trouble With Kim

I dreamt that I was dreaming and woke up next to my high school girlfriend who's facing the wall, away from me. I touch her shoulder to talk, to get comfort. She turns over and is blue and blistered and dead. I attempt to scream and get away but am stuck and mute—hissing rather than yelling. I cannot be heard and I cannot get away.

Last night I dreamed that my car falls into the left lane of the westbound Long Island Expressway next to Lefrak City and there are little bursts of fire on the right shoulder. I drive faster to get past this hazard but now fire is jumping up in the other lanes, and I floor the gas pedal—standing on the pedal. Now the raging fire flames high, as the windows are covering the entire road. I'm wondering how I continue to go straight without seeing the lines or the guardrail.

From the left lane I make out a manhole cover come loose and then fly off and land next to the hole. A Tyrannosaurus Rex climbs out of the hole and I pass it and it's eyes and head follow me as I pass and it lunges after me. Driving through the flames with my feet now lifted off the floor to avoid the heat, I see the monster galloping after me in the rear view mirror. Gaining on me.

I crash through barricades and am airborne and can't breathe. But his time the car falls slowly, swinging gently left and right like a feather cutting it's way through space and seeming to defy gravity.

I'm floating over small single-family houses in a residential neighborhood, side to side and come down on a tarp tied to a few trees and the car rips the tarp to the ground.

Then I'm in the yard, the tarp parachuting over the car, and then the tarp covers the car and it's mostly dark.

Last night I dreamed that I'm in apt. 4-A and everyone's dead and I hear keys jingling in the hallway. Then the teeth of the key crunching into the keyhole and the lock turning and the door opens and Kim walks in. He looks good and I'm filled with relief for a second then I freak out ... Insurance fraud, spent lawsuit money needing to be returned, my return to caring for a junkie. He smiles sheepishly at me and we hug for a long time. "I say what did you do?" I can smell his dirty clothes and feel his greasy hair. I'm freaking out as I hug my brother knowing that we've fucked up and would both probably be going to jail.

Last night I dreamed that I was at the counter in a bodega, with an onion and some beer, and I had no money to pay and I'm explaining to the guy in my shitty Spanish ... I'm explaining that I need to bring it to my mother who is dying, and I'll come back with money, and he's frowning and nodding and speaking faster than I can understand. My father comes from a door behind the counter like he works there and he smiles at me like this is all normal. I start crying and he say's "c'mere" and hugs me like I'm a little boy and he loves me, and can make me feel safe. In a way, I do.

In a dream I'm in Macys near the perfume counters and sitting on a mannequin's pedestal. There are people everywhere. Like it's Christmas, only busier. My mom is sitting next to me in a nightgown. I'm holding her hand and we're smiling at each other and looking into one another's eyes. I know she's leaving in a few seconds but I don't want to let her go. I know it's a dream but I don't want to wake up.

In bed and machine-gun III.

There's a large knife in my hand and I've just cut off my penis. I had a good reason but now I see that I hadn't thought it through. There's sharp pain and I've just ruined my life and I cannot do anything about it. I can't breathe.

I've killed someone in my dream. I cannot take it back. I stabbed them many times. I'm so sorry for the life they will miss out on. The people they loved and who loved them. I don't know who it is. I cannot remember. I'm so confused and horrified. I need to leave my parents, leave my friends, and never come back because I do not want to waste away in jail forever. I'll drive for a day and then take busses all the way to Bellingham. Then I'll live in the mountains—but I don't know how to live in the mountains. I don't know how to live. What have I done?

I'm on stage at P. S. 201 and I begin to play my white strat for the crowded auditorium. The intro to Boston's *Peace of Mind* and the room turns from talking amongst themselves to uproarious enthusiasm and loud cheering. I'm excited and continue. I pass the cue for the first verse and just keep on playing the opening riff, realizing that that's all I know. The crowd figures this out and I stop playing. Everyone is looking at me, disgusted. I'm horrified and want to hide.

I dreamed that I am in my parents Pomonok kitchen— the one in the project where I grew up and where they eventually got a washing machine. It blocked the window and took up all the space in between low cabinets on the left and on the right so you could only access that space by reaching into the cabinets next to them, the ones that weren't blocked.

So I'm using the surface on the right, chopping celery and the counter drops. It comes undone from the rear and side walls, and I'm assuming the cabinet below it has rotted and is no longer supporting it. It's rocking. I think Frankie can come and fix this for me (my friend Frankie is actually scheduled to come over my present day house to help with a few repairs). At the dinette table I ask Mom if she's moved the washer recently and she says no. She's in a nightgown. Dad and Kim are both there eating.

I dreamed that Kim was an only child and everything was fine. Then I came along and all the trouble in my family began. Both = bother.

I have my brother's severed head in my arms. I'm rocking it, feeling his curly hair withmy hands, his chin against my belly. I have to hide this forever or else I'll be in jail for life. I put it down—now in my childhood room I shared with him in the project. I ease it into a stiff plastic shopping bag from a local store. There are droplets of blood on the outside of the bag. I need a tissue to wipe it off. My life is over. Why did I do this?

I recently had a dream that I was in a kitchen and Kim walked in, white rice stuck around his mouth; he was quiet and knew his reappearance was bizarre but didn't know what to say. I hugged him and he hugged me, and I kissed the top of his head and cried—this time without thoughts of the trouble his reemergence would cause, (insurance money and social security and lawsuit payouts to repay, more work taking care of him, etc.).

I'm trying to cover up all of those trying to sleep in my bed. The apartment is like the one we had in Long Beach, but it's some other less polished beachside community, maybe Far Rockaway where I was born. Monika is in the bed and I worry that trying to cover her and make her warm will bother Jenn. I go looking in the closet for more blankets (harp is actually in bed with me this night!). I can't find any but then I see my mother (who's been dead for almost 15 years) and she's annoyed. I ask where the blankets are and she just glares and tells me my stuff is everywhere and charges away from me angrily stomping and saying I have to get my flicking shit off the porch. I see she's enraged and begin to say that *"shit"* is beginning to sell (it's now boxes of my CDs stored in a shed) and she dismisses that and charges toward the wall and says, "fuck!" So mad. So disappointed. So dismissive. *So my mother.*

I'm driving a van, a convertible van with the top down. Jenn's in the passenger seat and I'm looking high over my right shoulder at a kite I'm flying as I drive. Slack keeps appearing in the line and so I drive faster and hope for wind. The kite drops then rises and I'm barely breathing. This is the kite I never flew with my sons. This is the kite my father did fly with me, running along the road until he was coughing up yellow phlegm, looking up at the kite, tangled in the telephone cables above, knowing that the fun has ended before it began. I floor the gas pedal, and Jenn is light and happy, and we're suddenly in the air having driven off the end of the road. There's a thousand foot drop down to water and I'm holding the steering wheel with my left hand—my body lifted out of the seat now—and holding the kite with my right, looking at the kite. I know that even if it catches the wind, it can't hold me. It can't save me. But I won't let go. Jenn's gonna be so mad. I'm gonna die. My boys never flew a kite with their dad.

I'm on an elevator and a normal sized man gets on with a seven-foot tall woman with long, dark, curly hair, in a business suit. I can't stop staring. The man notices me looking at her (as must be the case whenever he's with *her*), but I can't stop. They get off the elevator and I remain on, wishing I had someone there with me to talk with about the woman.

I'm in a bathroom stall and flush and it overflows and won't stop. I'm standing in a growing puddle/flood of paper and shit.

Thank you.

GRAVE, 2002 - AGE THIRTY-SIX

A FEW WEEKS before my dad's last hospitalization, the one to rehab the hip he would break, the one where his heart would finally stop, I picked him up and drove him to Beth David Cemetery to visit Kim's grave. Mom had been urging him to go, to get some closure, to pay the respects that she was unable to make the trip for.

He'd aged years in the months since we buried his only other child, Dad's chip off the sad, old block. He was speaking in whispers now, and his only sparks of strength were spent on doing for Mom. He was done living, if it wasn't for bringing her cold drinks, helping her to the bathroom, sitting beside her, watching TV.

He didn't want to go with me. He asked what good it would do, that he had nothing to say. He was sure that it could not help, that he couldn't handle it.

It was early winter and I easily found the remote spot in the vast grid of oaks and stones. I'd been visiting. I held him under his free arm and he poked the ground with his cane as we walked over broken rocks and sad ivy, and when we came to the place where my grandmother lay, we stopped for a moment to pay respects and then stepped sideways to face the stone next to hers. Grandma Elsie had willed my brother a cemetery plot. We used to laugh at the morbidity of such a thing.

Seth Branitz

The inscription I'd commissioned reads:

BELOVED SON, BROTHER AND FRIEND.

LOVER OF MUSIC AND LAUGHTER.

The Russian guy at the tombstone store had sniggered when he read my application and said, "Lover? Dat's not correct English, yes? Lover is means like for woman. Right?" He kept looking at me as if I was up for such a critical edit. When he didn't move on, I asked him if there were different words in Russian that could be used to describe affection for things other than romantic love. Was the Russian word for romantic love romance-specific? And were strong positive feelings for other ideas and objects described using any other adjectives? Was there a single word that could be used to cover such a strong feeling of affection for many different, non-romantic things?

He didn't like my questions so henceforth I ignored his, and "Lover of music and laughter" it remained.

Stepping forward I said, "Hey big brother, look who's here."

I put my arm around Dad's shoulder and we were quiet.

It was chilly and life mostly sucked but I felt peaceful there, loving my father and creating this space for him to maybe love Kim for the last time.

One of the many cats that frequented the cemetery strode by and I kissed the air at her twice, she lifted her shoulder and walked on her toes, rubbed up sideways against a stone, and kept walking. If this was all there was to death, I thought, at least they have cats.

Maybe ten minutes passed and I wanted to go; I shuffled and squeezed Dad a little. He moved forward just a bit, straightened up and spoke, as if into a mic. "What didn't I do for you?"

Shit. I reminded him that this was not his fault.

"Of course it's my fault. I'm the father!"

I asked him not to do that but he couldn't help it.

We walked back to the car and held hands as I drove.

In the coming months and years I'd get a tiny bit of distance from the carousel of constant emergency that was this family. I eventually began to wonder if maybe it was true. Maybe it was, at least partially, my father's fault that my brother was dead. Maybe agreeing with the social workers to send him to Hawthorne (where he learned how to be a real delinquent from other, more seasoned juvenile criminals) drowned my brothers breaking heart and reminded him night after night that he was not welcome at home. That he was defective. Fragile Dad couldn't handle Kim's behavior and the baby (me) had to be their first priority now. I needed protection from him. I'm still not sure what he did to me. Maybe, because Dad's threshold for upset was retarded and his rage was central to his voice, this took the place of the love a son needs and deserves. Maybe this was all his son absorbed, leaving nothing to help him grow or to thrive. There was nothing to point him toward the light, nor the courage with which to push through, no vessel nor safe harbor.

No forgiveness.

No father.

Maybe it *was* his fucking fault.

I revisit this stuff so that I can get a percentage of the weight of these challenging memories off of my chest and out of my nightmares; to take this fodder I store for my next depression and burn it with last season's overgrowth. Start fresh.

I'm not sure it's working. In fact, its a rather brutal exercise, not only going back there, but seeing things I never thought to look at and light bulbs going on left and right, shining on bits and shadows that might have been better left at face value.

And I know that I am the one bearing the burden here. Dad is dead and will never be able to make it right. Kim is dead and will never be able to heal, to overcome his shortcomings. Mom, Tommy, Francis, Bobby, Lance—angels and demons flutter from my archives and beg to be reconciled, to be understood.

I labor to just *allow* life to be imperfect, tragic, or sad. Because, among other things, it is. How many people suffer over there as we rejoice over here and we know it yet we extract some sense of gratitude from our circumstances? And isn't this ok? If our joy were dependent on the end of all suffering, we'd be ruined.

I wonder if those who believe in an afterlife—where bliss is assured—are thus able to accept that suffering exists because they "know" that there will be peace before long, for them and hopefully for others. I see the appeal.

I think that for the rest of us, we just need to be available to help and to love when the opportunity presents itself, to soak up the rainbows as well as the rain and to keep a keen eye open for everything good, but for the most part our respective jobs and missions are more thoroughly and precisely fulfilled if we are able to be ok with life being imperfect. *With suffering.*

This somehow makes it easier to know that it sucked for Dad, and for Kim. They've suffered enough. So have you and I.

I look toward the abyss and although I can't exactly nail down what I feel, I imagine my father standing nearby, and I embrace him and say, "Its ok."

RICH, 2002 AGE – THIRTY-SEVEN

DURING THE LAST years of my brother's life, I had been party to his addiction and accompanying visits to detox, mental health professionals, lawyers, doctors and his fuck-head friends. I was in a role of constant mediator for him and his roommates, or our parents. For Mom and Dad I was chauffeur, cleaner, shopper, fixer, and advocate. I spoke weekly with insurance companies, pharmacies, housing management and hospitals.

We were poor. My mom had been poorer. My dad had gotten used to having little and while he hated it, he never seemed to aspire to, or work toward, greener pastures. The exception was his occasional and fleeting mention of how life would be better in Florida. I took it for granted that this was a possibility for us. His sister had done it with three kids. It hit me eventually that he was full of a particular brand of shit that was neither unscrupulous nor unforgivable. He was clueless and dreamed his dreams aloud. He would never save more than a couple hundred dollars. His employment prospects were limited. He couldn't bear the stress of ever moving again. I never liked the idea of moving myself, but used to hear Dad assert his dream with a measure of excitement. I was let down, as always, when I realized that Dad couldn't do anything right and we weren't going to Florida.

The year that my brother died, two novel things

happened for my family.

First, we found out that a long forgotten relative of my fathers, Cousin Lenny, had died. I'd never heard his name before, my father said that there had been something wrong with him. He hadn't seen or heard from him since they were kids. Lenny had apparently worked a menial job for the same company his entire life, lived simply and never married. A letter came to their home informing them that cousins would now be in receipt of a sum of money totaling around a thousand dollars each.

The next thing that happened was that I discovered that there is a place in Germany that bears our name, Branitz. There is also a Castle Branitz, and at the time I knew nothing of our connection to the place, or to the person or persons after whom they were named. It seems that this is along the border of Poland (and once actually was Poland) where my father's family comes from. My parents took delight in the discovery, my dad joking about the castle that he always felt somehow connected to the Rothschild family.

Our puny share of the inheritance went to pay for the headstone on Kim's grave. Thank you, cousin Lenny.

Dad spent a good amount of time away from my mom in the hospital during his last eight months. Her memory slipping and her illness causing her increasing and expanding pain, the issue of dispensing her medications became a huge issue. On one daily visit I saw her reach for her meds, saying she waited too long. I checked the jar, which I'd picked up the day before, and a month's dispensation was nearly gone.

Dad had developed a relationship with a pharmacist who would sometimes supply more meds than his prescriptions would warrant. I wasn't aware of this until the last year when I began to join Dad on his missions and run more and more of their errands on my own. It was harrowing to hear my seventy-eight year old father on the phone with Sam, the pharmacist, saying, "You have to. Please, man; *please.*" Sam braced himself when my dad would walk in for what had apparently turned into a long-time affair. Pleasantries done, they'd lower their voices and Dad's would rise above, "But she needs it. You don't understand, she NEEDS it."

With Dad in the hospital and my mothers habit now a fact of life, I took on the policing of her meds. I'd told Mom that she needed to back off of them and she said, "Why? Because I might OD? I'm *dying*, Seth!"

She was right. Hoping her deep, medicated sleeps would limit her consumption was a mistake, as her habit would interrupt sleep. I couldn't be there constantly to monitor her, and she was doing less and less for herself, so I needed to hire someone to stay with her.

Mom told me she didn't want someone with her if it wasn't me. I explained that the agency would not allow for her, in her advanced state of sickness, to be alone and that if we didn't have someone with her 24 hours a day, she would have to be in a hospital until such time as she would be moved to hospice. Mom said she wanted to die at home. I felt that this was impossible but tried. As it turned out, insurance would have paid for her to be in a hospital but would only supply short visits from nurses and aids. I pleaded with her to control her medication consumption, as I feared she would be forced into a hospital where I'd have no control over her care and her comfort, her privacy and her wishes. Dementia was affecting her ability to discern the passage of time and between that and her very real physical and emotional pain, she took far too many pills.

I was referred to an unlicensed home health aide from a woman in my parent's building. Tanya was from Soviet Georgia and upon meeting her at my mom's dinette table, she made a point to let me know she'd had it much better in the old country and that she worried about parking her car in our neighborhood. I said I was sorry to have wasted her time and opened the yellow pages to home health care agencies She apologized and proceeded to sell herself. We hired her as a stay-over when I couldn't be there, to manage and ration Mom's meds, and to oversee her basic needs.

This was 2002, and I'd been recovering from my own drug addiction since 1987. I hadn't felt vulnerable to temptation in many years, but I'd never been faced with this level of foundational disturbance. Taking care of my parents was in itself a strain the likes of which I'd never approached. I'd had no time to deal with the loss of my brother, and felt as if I was living in the shock I experienced immediately upon discovering that he was dead. The only comfort I could summon was in imagining the time when my mother would finally die, leaving me only to deal with Dad. I wanted relief, but availed myself of none of the conventional means of attaining a recharge or balance. I didn't have time to talk with trusted friends and didn't feel I deserved the right to complain. These were not my problems; they were my parent's. I was just there to help out. I wasn't exercising or sleeping enough. I'd fallen out of a formerly rewarding meditation routine. Even sex had been put off to another day, week, month when I wouldn't be so depressed, exhausted or preoccupied.

But when I reached into that bottle of Percocet, I wondered how good it might feel to lay down and relax. When I counted and recounted the Oxycontin, I imagined the absence of wide-eyed intensity, the soothing of my aching neck, the expanding of my wrenched back, and a short reprieve from the unfixable. It was all fucking hard and I was tempted to think that it could all get easier. What kept me from indulging was no moral fitness, it was the realization that without me as guardian, neither of my parents would have a chance. They could barely breathe after losing my brother, if I wasn't one hundred percent *on*, they'd lose me too. Also, they would never be reunited. So I felt it all, did all I could and kept the sinking boat afloat, while, at my hands, I watch my mother's physical and emotional affliction fade into a stupor.

Mom hated when I had to leave. I explained that I needed to tend to Dad, and that I needed to work a little in order to pay for her aide and to help with our bills. Her confusion surrounding Cousin Lenny and the discovery of Castle Branitz had her thinking that money had become a non-issue.

She said, "Wait, aren't we rich? We're rich, right?." It broke my heart to clarify. She'd been experiencing some form of relief with the thought that I would survive my family, free of worry, royal and rich.

One is eligible for hospice care when they've been determined to have six months or less to live but there appeared to be a sliding scale of acceptable pain management. Mom passed the six months although she wasn't getting better, just staying bad and getting more depressed as she had more time to suffer her losses. I negotiated with the hospice nurse again and again to increase her medication, and when the issue of her mismanaging pills came us, she insisted that mom needed someone there constantly. I resisted for as long as I could, and did what I had to do to ensure that she had a way to forget her pain, her sickness, and her horrible life, even if just for seconds at a time. It was awful and our bond grew in our suffering, Mom and me. Every night ended with a phone call. Every day ended with I love you.

STROKE, 2002 - AGE THIRTY-SIX

MOM WASN'T ANSWERING the phone.

Dad was rehabbing his broken hip at the place that was really a nursing home. Almost everyone there was elderly and not many were going to leave. His worst fear, he had said, would soon come true. And my brother could no longer look after her. So when I'd left mom in the morning, and she didn't answer the phone all afternoon and evening, I braced myself. I kept calling and I worried that she might have fallen. I worried that she might have done what we had discussed when she'd gotten her terminal diagnosis, when she was already in such acute pain that her waking hours had been reduced to only a few and those were spent on the couch, eyes closed, listening to the TV which stayed on 24/7, or to the transistor radio using ear buds.

I'd told her if it ever got so bad that the pain was inescapable or if she couldn't find any peace, any joy— and if she wanted to—I would help her to end the pain. But that I'd have to be absolutely sure she was clear about it. *Absolutely, completely sure.* I asked if she understood what I was saying. She stared off and said, "You want me to commit hari-kari," then turned slightly to look at me, and winked.

She told me that Dad and she had discussed this option but wouldn't do it to *me.* I told her not to worry about me, that I'd understand.

The Trouble With Kim

So the phone kept ringing and now maybe she'd gotten it done.

I drove the forty minutes to her and entered the apartment expecting to look directly to the left and see her on the couch where she had been passing her time in the company of The Nanny, CNN, and Oprah.

When I didn't see her I was momentarily relieved. Then as I closed the door my attention was drawn to the antique hall tree (a combination coat rack, bench and mirror) my mom had bought for $40 in 1953. Mom had refinished it and it was painted a distressed maroon and was as much a part of my growing up as the view from my bedroom window. I'd seen myself in its large, silvering inset mirror as many times as any, watched myself grow, at first standing on the bench to reflect, and eventually watching my head and shoulders get higher and higher above its bottom. In the dark I saw it, but in a few seconds I made out the ghost of my mom standing in front of it in her nightgown, hunched over and leaning with both hands on the armrests. I turned on the light and saw the rest. She was standing in a pool of sweat and piss, drenched and hyperventilating. Her arms and legs were quivering and she was grunting, as if trying to speak. She could neither move nor answer me.

Mom had asked me to do all I could to keep her at home. She wanted to have her last breath on her foam couch, listening to the TV or the radio, looking up at her many paintings and stone cherubs on her apricot walls. To call an ambulance would send her to the hospital and I couldn't guarantee that she'd ever make it home. If I called a neighbor, particularly in the middle of the night, they would certainly call 911. Nothing seemed right, but I had made a promise.

She was stuck. I sensed that she could hear me and that she just had no control over her body. I supposed that she'd been there for at least five hours, maybe more. She desperately needed to rest, but she was a in a sorry state. It was probably a stroke.

I got the shower going, and after realizing there was no easy way, I began to inch her toward the bathroom. She was breathing heavy and speaking only in repetitive syllables, I lifted her still obese body over the side of the tub and got her clean. I felt her shame and her psychic resistance. This was one of the most physically challenging experiences of my life and I had no room to consider the other ways this might affect me, or her. *But it did.* This was added to the list of "things a son should not ever have to do," by my mother-in-law after that night.

It must have taken an hour.

Eventually I got her back to her couch, clean, dry and in clean nightclothes. She fell asleep, eyes partly open and face half twisted.

She lived another few weeks without speaking or eating, and as her weight plummeted, her false teeth no longer fit. Without her bridge she looked ancient, chin jutting out and lips caved in over her gums. She stared at the ceiling and I looked for meaning in the way she squeezed my hand. She would seem to try to say something and tense up, and I'd get close then she'd just go limp, exhausted—both of us helpless to make this a two-way conversation.

I think she wanted to tell me something important; to ask about Dad. I told her Dad was doing great. His hip was almost all healed and he was feeling good. Bullshit. Maybe she was trying to tell me how to manage some small detail of the housekeeping, or of the lawsuit, or of her pain.

One day, holding hands and watching Seinfeld, she squeezed very tightly and tugged a little. Her body tensed and she began grunting. I thought she might be having a seizure. I thought she might die right then. I stood over her and said MOM, WHAT? WHATS WRONG? What do you NEED?

Her free hand came up and clenched my shoulder and she pulled me down to within inches of her face, her mouth and eyes now wide.

She fixed her eyes on mine and in five distinct sentences and one extended exhale she said,

"I love you. I love you. I love you. I love you. I love you."

I'd stopped breathing now and her eyes softened and drifted back off into nowhere. She let herself slowly back down to the couch and relaxed.

She never spoke again.

She had used every last bit of strength to attend to the detail she found most pressing.

In a file in my brain along with all the insistent memories that I'm attempting to let go of, there is this one thing I choose not to forget.

First she had me. Then she spoke these words. What happened in-between dulls in comparison. Of this I will never let go.

The antique hall-tree stands just inside the front entrance to my home. It gets a lot of use as a depository for hats, coats, book bags and other items I constantly wish would be put away properly.

For a few years, my wife and sons and I referred to it as "the coat rack," "the bench," "the purple thing," "the thing," and finally settled on an identifier that would for, practical reasons, but with no shortage of pause and irony, make life simpler.

We call it, "Eve."

A Bit About Mom

MY MOTHER HAD no awards, no riches, no degrees, nor money. She wasn't fit or particularly personable, but she was an artist and somehow that always seemed good enough.

She'd point out the lines of cable strung overhead. Distinct greens of different houseplants and vegetables, and the length of a ladies neck; Modigliani necks, she called them. We'd watch Van Gogh sunsets over Cezanne skylines from our fourth-floor window in the project in Queens. She seemed to have a third eye, not attached to her mind as the other two, but this one wired directly to her artist-soul.

She grew up poor and rather poor she remained, and she always hesitated to indulge in nice things even when she could.

When she was diagnosed with stage-four lung cancer— her third bout with cancer in five years—she told me that she wanted the very simplest and cheapest coffin, just a plain pine box. "That's how Jews do it," she said. There's no heaven. When you're dead you're dead. Spend no more money than necessary.

She'd had a hard life...

She'd been burned in a fire at five after she'd waved her comb over a candle by which her mother was doing her hair. Her mother died when my mom was only thirteen.

She told me about her father who sat sobbing at the table during the Great Depression, head in hands with her mother standing over him yelling WE NEED FOOD! *Go get FOOD!*

Then engaged in her teens to a nice, financially responsible guy. Life was finally getting better and then he fucking hit her. She left.

There was the Miami she travelled to on a bus and where she worked and swam, and dated and painted, and didn't have to brace herself for the New York winters, or for her now arrested low self-esteem, and from where she travelled to visit her widowed father in the Bronx, and stayed. The life of *her* choosing, gone.

My dad spent half of my childhood in hospitals and most of the rest in a bathrobe. Mom was just slightly less depressive but the two of them were well stocked with mix-and-match head-meds they'd use, and abuse, and occasionally overdose on. My brother challenged, worried, and infuriated her from the time I was born right up until his suicide. *And then some more.*

When I was eight and wanted a cat, she refused. She was scared of cats and they were expensive to care for. But with dad's help, she eventually caved in and tiny Sam came home. A few mornings later, I woke up and came out of my room and there was Mom, kneeling beside the chair, cautiously petting the little sleeping fur ball. This is one of my only happy memories from childhood, all of which feature animals.

She always said she was terrified of dogs. After she died I found a picture of her, probably as a teenager, clearly delighted and beautifully content, two puppies in her arms.

Once Mom was painting my dressers red in the living room and the cat leapt onto the project and immediately off, tracking red footprints across the desk and the floor. She cleaned the cat and the floor; but left the red paw prints on the desk.

My mother was the only person I knew who liked radio more than TV. She was always listening, absorbing, hating, admiring— distracted and inspired. She often quoted one of her on-air heroes: Bernard Meltzer, Curtis Sliwa, Lynn Samuels, Garrison Keeler, and Howard Stern among them. She said that radio was more intimate and varied and that it never stopped moving. Short order medicine for all-day suffering.

As a teen, I'd come in and kiss her and she'd say, "STOP! Kiss me again." And I'd walk toward her, holding my breath. As I'd kiss her cheek, I'd hear the sound of her sniffing. Busted. And I'd do my best to lie about why I smelled like weed, beer, or what have you.

Stories of The Holocaust shocked and tormented her as if it had happened to *her*. She was obsessed. There never seemed to be a Channel Thirteen special on the war, or on concentration camps, that we missed. As a boy, I too watched these black-and-white people whose faces looked to be equal parts my face and death, and it fucked *me* up. So I get it. She ran the stories over and over and made it the present. Growing up during the depression and WW2 she felt as if she'd just missed death by an inch. Her terror persisted, like just missing being slammed dead by a speeding bus when mindlessly stepping into its way in the street, heart exploding, only six million times more horrible.

Here and now, at her weakest, her darkest moment came on 9/11. Watching her in front of the screen I wondered how many people just died there in front of their televisions.

In her final sickness the only thing to do for her was to be there. Things were as awful as could be, save for me being healthy and able to help.

She was crumbling, but she was my rock, the only one I'd call when I couldn't see a way out of my own pile of suffering. She'd listen to me. She didn't have the right thing to say, the cash for rent or the ride to rehab, but she'd listen, and I'd talk. I'd say how hard life was and she'd concur. Then together, over the phone, we'd cry.

From her I learned to notice. Even in my most grim moments I see color in darkness. I hear harmony in thunder.

Near the end she got very controlling. The dying do this; try to control what they can. It was, after all, totally out of her control now.

The last time she mentioned the coffin thing she said, "You remember now, I've told you that I want the cheapest box? The very cheapest, plainest one?"

Yes, mom. You told me.

"Well, I've changed my mind. I want the next one up."

We both smiled a toast to futility, to irony, to Woody Allen and to our love for one another.

I wish she had taken comparable care of herself when she was well.

But that day I was proud of her.

She was buried just over a month later, eight and a half months after my brother, twelve days after my dad, on a Matisse morning, under a Chagall sky, in the second cheapest coffin money could buy.

RECAP

Kim died 8/1/01

Dad died 4/12/02

Mom died 4/24/02

SUSAN, 2002 - AGE THIRTY-SIX

MY MOTHER'S FRIEND, Alice, lived in the project, just a few buildings away, across Jewel Avenue. They'd become friends on the Lower East Side in a development called The Lavenburgs while they were both very young mothers. They'd migrated to Queens around the same time and we visited their apartment more often than they visited ours.

Alice played piano and sang with smoky, groggy power—Yiddish songs mostly. She and Mom would talk in the dinette for hours while I alternately watched network television and tooled around at the piano.

Alice's younger daughter, Susan, was born in 1954, the same year as my brother. As children in Manhattan, they were friends, since our mothers spent a lot of time together. Once both families had migrated to Queens, Susan and Kim continued for a while, perhaps more than friends, though I'll never be sure. Their teens drew them to other interests and colleges.

The first time I knew something was wrong with Susan was when I was eight, and she was eighteen. Our mothers were talking in our dinette, and I found myself alone in my room with Sue. As I showed her a few of my model cars and flipped through one of my sketchpads, I could see in my peripheral vision that she was sticking her chest out and leaning into me. Just before her chest touched me, I turned to face her and leaned away, to which she burst into laughter. Not knowing what to do, I resumed the tour, but each time I did, she threw her elbows back, her rib cage and sizable tits forward, and bent toward me. I jumped back, looking at her face, and again she cracked up laughing. She did this several times without ever saying a word and I wasn't sure what she was doing. Was she showing them off? Did she want me to touch them, as I'd recently learned was a thing after flipping though a couple of bizarre magazines I'd found under my brother's mattress? I excused myself to the room where our moms must have been enjoying the sound of distant laughter, and stayed close to them for the remainder of the visit. I decided never to be alone with Susan again.

I didn't tell anybody about this incident. I didn't understand it and wouldn't have known how to explain it.

Over the years my mother and I ran into Susan in the neighborhood and she was stranger each time, eventually crossing the line from weird into fucked-up. Alice told my mother that Susan had moved out and was showing up only occasionally for money. When my mother asked Marsha about her, the elder sister nodded her head in resignation.

We passed by her one day as she sat—a beautiful hippie leaning against a tree. Mom asked how she'd been and she told us that she had gotten pregnant and had given birth to a boy who she'd given up for adoption. She smiled and ranted for the entire telling, pausing only for a reaction after saying that the father had been black. My mother was unprepared to respond and just said, "Take care of yourself, darling," squeezed my hand and pulled me along.

Throughout my teens, Susan was one of a few unfortunate men and women who sat near the supermarket begging for money. She got dirtier and less pretty by the year but always said hi to me and I'd smile or wave.

No stranger to crazy, I never thought to distinguish one odd person from the other with diagnosis or hyperbole, but was more interested in how I fit into their vacuum. Starting at home, we'd had social workers, shrinks, shock therapy, shame, cops at the door, violence, Valium and Long Island Ice Tea breakfasts. We had neighbors eating out of dumpsters, turning tricks in apartment 7-A , screaming "Jesus" into neighbors' windows at midnight, and leaping off the Verrazano Bridge. Acid teens were beginning to fade but crack was heating up and as I watched, as I cultivated my own pet perversions, I felt both infinitely isolated, and more at one with the craziest of them.

I developed strategies to guard myself from those who would suck the vitality from my stride, but I still had a kindred interconnection with them, whether they were aware of it or not.

Susan was my family. She was one square in the patchwork of lower east side heartbreak that shrouded my family and hers.

She eventually ceased to acknowledge me and so I just kept my eyes straight ahead, or went the long way around her and her ever-growing altar of garbage and shame.

The day my father died, I went to my catatonic mother and whispered in her ear, "Dad's doing better. He loves you and will see you soon." Then I left her in the care of an aide, walked the bend in Kissena Boulevard and crossed the street to a luncheonette where Dad and I had spent many mornings during my youth. I heard my dad's voice emerge from my lips as I ordered, "a couple poached eggs, well done rye toast and coffee," at the counter—one foot in childhood, the other in the ruthless current of manhood—ate half of it, and left.

Through the door and to the right, a woman sat cross-legged on a large charcoal blanket next to a shopping cart full of paper and rags. Her face was turned down and she was mumbling. A few steps from the luncheonette, I saw that I knew her. I approached, and said, "Good morning." She turned her face slightly up, her cheeks blotchy red and so bloated that her head seemed spherical, her eyes barely open, her lips swollen and badly cracked. I could smell piss and sweat from ten feet away and stood looking into her face for a few moments, hoping for something other than this. I asked, "What's your name?" The two syllables she grunted were unmistakably, "Susan." I said, "I'm Seth." If she smiled, I couldn't tell and I sadly accepted that this was no reunion. As I stepped away, I thought that, amid her mumbled words, I heard her say, "Sorry."

I called her sister, Marsha, a couple of weeks later to let he know what had happened to my family. It had been a few years since we'd connected and I liked her at least as much as some of my blood relations. She fell silent for a bit and the said, "Seth, I can't believe you're telling me this. Susan just died." That same week as my father had, in fact.

Seth Branitz

The same week that I saw her. Marsha had been in and out of touch with her mentally ill sister for many years, had had to wash her hands of her, as there was nothing to be done for someone as far gone as Susan had been. Neither Marsha nor I were in any position to offer one another much support, but there was a hint of comfort, not only in our shared familial sadness, but the dark truths that we both now found ourselves orphans and only children.

I wonder about the concentration of bitterness in my family of origin, and if it's either genetically predisposed or karmic. Then I look at how it's extended beyond my bloodline and into the lives of so many close to us, and I wonder if it wasn't due to some localized curse, faulty programming or something funky in the water. But when I take the time, when I scan the lives of people who live beyond our proximity and lineage, I can see that pain has no preference for the particular likes of us. Life finds the same shitty prospects within spitting distance of us all, just like joy. I probably shouldn't, but I find both prospects somehow encouraging.

Epilogue

GRATITUDE DOES NOT come automatically to one who waits for the next tragic phone call. To one who spent years defending their intellectual stand for expecting the worst. It takes a forced statement or mediation on something "else." And it often takes what feels like heroic effort. To risk life and limb and search and rescue gems that hide behind my habit of hustle, strive, fail, justify and criticize. To indulge in a break from momentum and trust that there will be a reward. I'm sure that's a critical part of the secret for people who aren't graced with automatic sunshine. To search for the glorious and the adorable in the mundane and the sucky. I know beautiful things are everywhere, likely in greater abundance than the other crap. I know because I've taken to this practice on and off for a good part of my life. I aspire for this to develop into less of a job and more of a default. To exchange my minds old, cruddy filters with fresh and more permeable ones that allow rose-colored everything to breathe through, and to develop my ability to mine pebbles of fortune from the rubble of my regret. That soothes me. That saves me.

A painless world tempts me. It used to be an urging, a blaring call to simplify and to escape. I would drive faster, take more, breathe less, visit places where people die regularly and I would say, 'What will be will be." I've balanced on the ledge, careened toward the wall and clenched the lethal dose in my clammy palm.

An insidious seduction, this stuff of quitters and settlers and no-shows and soul thieves. I don't think I'm perfectly immune to its seduction, but I'm no longer impressed. I see escape as a long, hot bath before all virtue winds down the drain along with suds and pubic hairs and grime, overflowing and finding its way down and down and all over the place, leaving the house soft and rotten. I've lived in such a house. I've played that movie through to the credits and the ironic outtakes, and I've suffered the loss of more than a few escape artists, some of whom I love. One being my brother.

We're all worried. We all hate. And we all have deeply beautiful stories. We keep them hidden and they contort us and abuse us and enslave us and lie.

I'm not over the people I've lost. I'm regularly considering those I might eventually be losing. Then and now I scream at the news of those who took their lives and left our hearts a mushroom cloud.

I'm now wholly certain that there are no specific prerequisite shortcomings. One needn't have an addiction, a diagnosis, a prescription, a maligned gene, an insane parent, or a tragic episode to suffer misconceptions about their worth, or about the nature of this 'human' business. Some of us simply find ourselves alone.

The bleeders, loud mouths and misbehavers get our attention, but the quietly hurting are the majority. The sufferings which we lock behind our smiles are acid for our hearts.

The Trouble With Kim

I don't know what it is that managed to keep ME afloat day-after-day when I saw no future and despised my present. I knew that I had potential, but it appeared as a yearning, not as a goal. This moment, one of aspiring fulfillment, wasn't on the horizon. Maybe it was that I saw that my parents would surely die if I left just as they did when my brother took *his* life. I despised that responsibly but honored it nonetheless. Maybe it helped that I dumped my guts onto lined paper and guitar strings and that very thing became my promise. That something about me knew it wasn't about me and that my suffering wasn't as important to the world as my light. Maybe it was the people who love me and hold me up when I'm wobbly and stupid. Maybe I'm just afraid of the drastic change.

I'm thankful for whatever modicum of moral discernment allowed me to hold the gun but not pull the trigger, to taste the poison but finally spit.

When I allow my mind to run, I'm beaten. I see no way out.

But when I serve and create, build and connect, I glide.

It consumes me and defies logic and responsibility, and I think that anyone who abuses themselves inwardly or outwardly and realizes it (but doesn't stop) is, by and large, an abuser, if not an addict. Junkies get all the attention, but addicts are everywhere.

And addicts are like zombies. Not bad. Just starving.

Now it's different. I worry that the life that *I know is a gift*, might end tomorrow or today, and I play through the delivery of the news. I envision the spread of surprise and the grief of my dear ones.

And then I play though the eventual moments of light. Of them getting over it. Of them getting back to their lives. All the natural and appropriate stages of mourning. But unnaturally experienced *by me* and *for me* prematurely. I'm grieving my own mortality. My own actual demise.

Before I fall off to dreamland, I worry and I calculate and I stand in the blinding chill of my middle age and I fucking hate it. I consider the next friend, write the next sentence, hum the next line, and pray to whatever good there is in the universe that I can bask long enough in its beam to do something worthwhile. Pretty stressful shit.

So thank you. Not God. Not sure about her, no offense. But thank you, world, for including me. For Good, because I do believe in Good. Thank you. Thank you for breath in, and breath out. For purring animals who invade my space and needy people who don't. For Catskill mountains majesty. For community, language, laughter and harmony. For those who listen and for those who I ignore. For hope-fiends and dreamers, annoying and sweet. For the Internet and for books. For each chance to start again. For my body and for yours. For this ocean of gifts which seems to be an almost constant struggle. For taking less for granted. For taking more to heart. For all that's blissful and for all that's awful.

I am a fortunate man; thanks for reading.